"Daniel Priestley is one of our most popular guests to talk about entrepreneurship on The Diary of a CEO. He offers clear, practical guidance for adopting an entrepreneurial mindset and starting and growing business. In *Lifestyle Business Playbook*, he explains how to understand the big trends and then lays out bold, clear steps to building a business that serves your life, not the other way around. This isn't theory - it's a distillation of real entrepreneurial wins, losses, and wisdom. If you want a business that gives you freedom, purpose, and profit, this is the book you've been waiting for."

—**Steven Bartlett**, Entrepreneur, Investor &
Host of The Diary of a CEO Podcast

'If you want a business that gives you freedom, purpose, and profit, this is the book you've been waiting for.'
STEVEN BARTLETT, DIARY OF A CEO

LIFESTYLE BUSINESS PLAYBOOK

HOW TO HAVE FUN, FREEDOM AND FULFILMENT WITH YOUR OWN BUSINESS

DANIEL PRIESTLEY

CAPSTONE
A Wiley Brand

This edition first published 2026
© 2026 Daniel Priestley

The right of Daniel Priestley to be identified as the author of this work has been asserted in accordance with law.

Registered Offices

John Wiley & Sons, Inc., 111 River Street, Hoboken, NJ 07030, USA

John Wiley & Sons Ltd, New Era House, 8 Oldlands Way, Bognor Regis, West Sussex, PO22 9NQ, UK

For details of our global editorial offices, customer services, and more information about Wiley products visit us at www.wiley.com.

The manufacturer's authorized representative according to the EU General Product Safety Regulation is Wiley-VCH GmbH, Boschstr. 12, 69469 Weinheim, Germany, e-mail: Product_Safety@wiley.com.

Wiley also publishes its books in a variety of electronic formats and by print-on-demand. Some content that appears in standard print versions of this book may not be available in other formats.

Limit of Liability/Disclaimer of Warranty
While the publisher and the authors have used their best efforts in preparing this work, including a review of the content of the work, neither the publisher nor the authors make any representations or warranties with respect to the accuracy or completeness of the contents of this work and specifically disclaim all warranties, including without limitation any implied warranties of merchantability or fitness for a particular purpose. Certain AI systems have been used in the creation of this work. No warranty may be created or extended by sales representatives, written sales materials or promotional statements for this work. The fact that an organization, website, or product is referred to in this work as a citation and/or potential source of further information does not mean that the publisher and authors endorse the information or services the organization, website, or product may provide or recommendations it may make. This work is sold with the understanding that the publisher is not engaged in rendering professional services. The advice and strategies contained herein may not be suitable for your situation. You should consult with a specialist where appropriate. Further, readers should be aware that websites listed in this work may have changed or disappeared between when this work was written and when it is read. Neither the publisher nor authors shall be liable for any loss of profit or any other commercial damages, including but not limited to special, incidental, consequential, or other damages.

Library of Congress Cataloging-in-Publication Data
Names: Priestley, Daniel, author.
Title: Lifestyle business playbook / Daniel Priestley.
Description: Hoboken, NJ : Wiley, 2026. | Includes index.
Identifiers: LCCN 2025033017 (print) | LCCN 2025033018 (ebook) | ISBN 9780857089922 (paperback) | ISBN 9780857089946 (adobe pdf) | ISBN 9780857089939 (epub)
Subjects: LCSH: New business enterprises. | Entrepreneurship. | Work environment. | Industrial management.
Classification: LCC HD62.5 .P676 2026 (print) | LCC HD62.5 (ebook)
LC record available at https://lccn.loc.gov/2025033017
LC ebook record available at https://lccn.loc.gov/2025033018

Cover Design: Wiley
Cover Image: © Nazia/stock.adobe.com

Set in 11/16 pt and Adobe Jenson Pro by Straive, Chennai, India
Printed and bound by CPI Group (UK) Ltd, Croydon, CR0 4YY

C9780857089922_071125

I dedicate this book to my dad who role-modeled to me a lifestyle and a way of doing business based on kindness, humility and service to others.

CONTENTS

INTRODUCTION

SMALL TEAMS HAVE INFINITE LEVERAGE NOW

There are businesses that are built to deliver fun, freedom and fulfilment. The people who run these businesses get to live their lives in a way no human has ever lived before. They can live and work from anywhere – their wealth and income isn't linked to the time they spend in a given workplace; they don't need to own and maintain physical assets in any particular location. The assets they create are digital – they transcend geographical boundaries, are impervious to decay and deliver value at any scale. The more of these digital assets you create, the more you will have a business that sets you free.

These businesses are often called lifestyle businesses. They aren't like the businesses of the past that were built to deliver profit to offset the pain and drudgery that had to be endured. A lifestyle business is able to pump out profit and passion. It makes money and it's meaningful. It's valuable and it fuels your vitality.

I have a lifestyle business. In any given month I might find myself getting paid to attend a rooftop pool party in Dubai, doing a podcast in LA with someone I massively admire, hosting a team retreat in Portugal, taking a big group of clients skiing in the Italian Alps or flying to Bucharest with my co-founder to talk to a group of thousands of cool creative types. All of these things happen so regularly that I often have to turn down amazing experiences because I'm already booked to do something else that's mind blowing.

At the same time, I get to work from my home office, I drop my kids to school most mornings, have regular date-nights with my wife, get several fitness training sessions in a week, go on long walks in nature and enjoy fantastic lunches with my mentors. How is it possible that this is my life? At what other time in history would it be possible to live this way? I'm not special. I have no qualifications. I don't have rich parents. I do not possess genius-level intelligence or mesmerizing good looks.

The only thing I have leveraged is an awareness that we are living through a special time in history.

Mind you, I didn't arrive here on a smooth path. I boomed and busted three times before I was 35. Each time was a gut-wrenching roller-coaster ride. Each time I started with nothing, quickly built, discovered a fatal error and fell flat on my face.

At 21, I quit my job working for my mentor. I had no money but I'd learned a lot about marketing and sales campaigns so I put all of the startup costs on my credit cards. The business got off to a strong start and did over a million in its first year running campaigns in the financial services industry. No sooner had we taken off, a change in regulations forced our clients to change the way they could advertise and everything got put on pause. I pivoted the business to marketing franchises and created a partnership with a franchisor expanding nationally.

At 24, they offered me $14 million for the business I'd started just three years earlier. The negotiations revealed our values were not aligned; we ended up having a massive fight in their boardroom and the deal was off and with it was my biggest-paying client. I found myself the day before Christmas drinking heavily in the realization that I was back to square one with no plan and serious financial pressures. I had put everything I had into the growth of someone else's brand and now had nothing to show for it.

The following year I rebuilt from scratch. I moved to London and began promoting two international speakers and best-selling authors as their agent in the UK. Things were flying, only to get wiped out by the global financial crisis. One minute I was running campaigns that made $500,000 in a week and living in a luxury penthouse, then the following year I was living in my sister's spare room and maxing out my credit cards just to live. My business was totally reliant on other people's personal brands and ideas. My company was great at marketing and sales but we didn't have assets of our own and when those partnerships stopped, the whole business crashed.

The third wipe-out was particularly painful. I rebuilt after the 2009 financial crisis and once again got off to a fast start. I opened offices in London, Singapore, Melbourne and Tampa. Everywhere we went, our launch campaigns created explosive sales and I thought the rocket ship was finally heading to the stars. I flew back into London and found that my financial director was waiting for me in the office telling me that our UK business was borderline solvent and he was going to quit. Then my UK team of 10 people took me to breakfast, threatening to all quit that day as well.

While I'd been away, the business had run into the ground under the watch of the people I'd put in charge. I was forced to choose to take on a massive loan or to let the whole business topple again. We were showing such promise so I decided to take on the loan. With a newborn baby at home I signed up to take on 60 months of payments neither the business or I could afford. It would take every ounce of me to stay sane during the next five years as all the spare money I had went straight out the door. I barely paid myself anything, I took on consulting work at night and agreed to write books I didn't have time to write. I would travel for hours to do a quick speaking gig if it would lead to even a marginal amount of cash in the bank that month.

By the time I finished paying the loan off, I had three kids under five and I was objectively a wreck. I was a workaholic, I'd neglected my health and put on 10 kg. I was consumed with anger and resentment every month when the loan payment went out. I wasn't being a great husband or father but I was blessed with a wife who stuck it through with me and never wavered. I paid a high price but I'd rescued the business, we'd built solid foundations for future success and was on the other side of this five-year financial marathon – finally it was time to channel those monthly payments into the growth of the business and then start paying myself properly.

The final payment for the loan was in early March 2020. The relief in paying that last payment actually made me tear up. It took five years of payments but now I was free. Or so I thought for a few weeks; there would be another challenge to face. Three weeks after making the final payment, the UK went into lockdown. My entire business revolved around live events and workshops and now everyone had to stay at home. I had hundreds of clients due to start with us in April and no way to deliver what they'd paid for.

The team who had ridden with me through the ups and downs looked into my eyes bewildered as I told them all that every employee except one would be put on the furlough scheme – basically their employment would be put on pause and it would be against the rules for them to help me.

We had faced so much together and now I was telling them they weren't allowed to do anything; they had to log out of their e-mail accounts and sit at home. I stared at their faces on Zoom and I did my best to put on a confident, matter-of-fact face; internally I felt like I had betrayed their loyalty. I had no idea how this was going to work out.

A few of us spent the next six months rebuilding the business to run digitally. I was already a workaholic, I already suffered chronic stress and I had dealt with hemorrhaging cash flow for years. This felt familiar territory but it also felt like I was getting very close to destroying myself. My business career was not exactly a lifestyle up until this point.

This last push was the one that changed everything. Through each of my booms and subsequent busts I had learned valuable lessons. I discovered the power of building my own personal brand instead of being reliant on others. I learned the power of owning my own ideas and turning them into assets. I'd discovered how to make marketing and sales perform urgently and under pressure. I'd learned how to make a business churn out consistent cash. I had learned how to build and leverage digital assets. Then the Covid-19 lockdowns became the impetuous for me to bring it all together and build businesses in a different way – robust, profitable and flexible.

I discovered all of the pain, stress and volatility had prepared me pretty well for the trends that converged in that moment. The lessons and strategies I learned in that journey and share in this book are perfect for the times we are in. If you're prepared to shift your thinking and act strategically, you don't have to ride the ups and downs – you can skip straight to the part where business is fun and fulfilling.

You are living through a unique time.

At rare moments in history the entire system changes. The last time this happened was when the Agricultural Age gave way to the Industrial Age. Most humans went from working on the land, producing food and serving the landed gentry, to working in factories or offices, producing goods and services and serving large corporations and the national tax office. This was made possible because of steam power, breakthroughs in steel and iron, electricity and combustion engines and nation-states that could more easily trade than fight.

HUH... 7 HOURS TO GO...

The businesses that emerged during the Industrial Age revolved around standardized components. Factories developed standardized processes using standardized machinery and parts to produce standardized products and services. These businesses needed humans to be components in the machine and we developed standardized labour for standardized pay. The way the economy was set up reflected the dominant technology that it ran on.

Today's technology dictates a different type of economy in formation. The Industrial Age technology took us beyond the limits of our biological muscles and brute strength – cars replaced horses and tractors replaced farmhands. Digital technology takes us beyond out natural limits of communication and intelligence. Digital technology isn't confined to any place – it's decentralized. It doesn't break down with use – it self-replicates flawlessly, infinitely. It doesn't require costly maintenance – once created, it costs almost nothing to store, move or use. The economy is reorganizing around the new attributes of this dominant technology.

Old businesses are centralized – they decay and require endless maintenance that must be paid for with endless growth. New businesses are able to operate anywhere, anytime, forever, at low cost.

The old type of businesses are going to be replaced by this new type of businesses. You are at the forefront of this trend and you have the ability to live a life that would seem beyond magical to any of your ancestors.

The traditional businesses of the last 200 years weren't fuelled by human spirit. Genuine human spirit had to be parked outside so that jobs could be done. Sitting in a cubicle wasn't an entirely weird way to spend your days. Fighting off the will to sleep, scream or walk away was just a normal

part of going to work. The new businesses run on vitality –
the irreplaceable life force we all possess. Anything that isn't
based on pure human energy will soon be done by computers or robots. The more your life is repetitive drudgery, the
less you will earn because technology can do it better, faster,
cheaper and safer than you. The more you do things that are
playful, silly, fun, wild, adventurous, creative and messy, the
more you will be able to earn – if you know how to structure
it into a lifestyle business.

These changes were all happening slowly and then two
things happened in the early 2020s. The Covid-19 lockdowns showed the world that most jobs could be done from
anywhere. Then ChatGPT showed the world that most
jobs could be done with AI.

In the 2010s, faster and faster internet, cloud computing
and social media began to open up a world of new opportunities. The smartphone democratized the ability to create
media and have super computers everywhere, banks went
online and cryptocurrencies emerged as a low-friction way
to transfer value across borders. The disruptive technology
was in place but the way we worked hadn't changed much –
most people still felt they had to go to a fixed place of work
in order to get anything done.

Then came Covid-19. Governments all over the world
shut down their economies, locked people in their homes
and pumped trillions of dollars into the system with almost
no rules or conditions attached. In one fell swoop they normalized working remotely, buying online, getting things
delivered virtually or by post. All at once we didn't have

a choice to do things the conventional way, we all had to figure out how our lives would work doing almost everything online. We didn't just buy our groceries online and consume more podcasts, we started hosting cocktail parties online, getting live guitar lessons from someone on the other side of the world, conferencing with industry leaders by talking on our phones. We discovered all sorts of products and services could function even with everyone being stuck at home.

The stage was suddenly set. The economy was ready and willing to do things differently. There was more money flowing around than ever before, more technology in people hands, a willingness to connect with people remotely and huge problems that needed solving.

Then in late 2022, along came the launch of ChatGPT and for the first time millions of people woke up to the power of large language models (LLMs). We added a new layer of computing power that could augment human creativity, innovation and reach. Everyone suddenly had access to a basic lawyer, life-coach, management consultant, marketing assistant, health advisor, software developer, solutions architect and graphic designer. Our jaws collectively hit the floor every time the AI models got an upgrade and we could witness it doing more and more advanced tasks in a heartbeat for free. Some of the most highly paid traditional jobs were suddenly put on notice – this thing will soon do 90% of your job for free!

Suddenly the world lurched violently towards a new way of doing things, and one of the byproducts was the birth of the lifestyle business.

A lifestyle business has three elements that make it unique.

☐ *Creative freedom* – the ability to work on projects you are passionate about and say no to work that is not right for you. The ability to do something a little strange, for a niche community on a timescale that suits you. This is made possible because over 70% of the world's population has access to fast internet and has organized themselves into niche online communities and common interest groups. The ability to tap into these groups allows you to make money from things that were previously considered too weird, nuanced or esoteric to be commercially viable.

☐ *Location freedom* – the ability to live and work from anywhere and to move when you chose. The ability to serve your customers no matter where they are in the world. This is made possible thanks to cloud computing, software as a service and ubiquitous fast internet. It's also acceptable thanks to Covid-19, which rapidly normalized remote working and online shopping.

☐ *Time freedom* – the ability to structure your day (or night) the way you choose without the pressure of having a direct relationship between your time working and the money you earn. This is made possible by the countless ways you can create a product or service that is available online.

A lifestyle business isn't only possible right now, it's probably a safer and more sustainable option than a career working for large corporations. Millions of people are already exploring their options to have more fun, freedom and fulfilment.

Large corporations are losing their power. It used to be the case that smart, talented people went to work in big organizations because that's where they could earn the most money, get job security and learn new skills fastest.

Today it's the opposite of what people experience. Large corporations pay people a basic average of what they are worth based on a market rate. Highly skilled and talented people get overlooked or excluded because they don't fit with an arbitrary human resources (HR) policy. Big companies have become hostile environments for anyone who likes to get things done fast without the office politics. Big companies often hire large numbers of workers to fulfil jobs they later perceive they don't need. Then when they realize their folly they often fire large swathes of workers to get their profit margins back in line with expectations. It's not a fun environment for those that get sent packing or those who get to stay.

Large organizations regularly deploy workers into projects that make no sense to anyone on the ground while ignoring the sensible recommendations of people who are actually working closely with paying customers. Asking for time off can be like negotiating a divorce; working remotely comes with spyware that tracks how many mouse-clicks you do each hour; and if you work in the office you pay inflated rent and endure a dehumanizing daily commute. No one in their right mind wants to work this way once they know how good the alternatives are.

So what's the alternative? Imagine earning more money than you could work in corporate, while living or travelling wherever you like and only working on projects that excite and delight you and others.

All of this is conditional on being set up to do business in a way that leverages the new technological and societal landscape. You can't play by the old rules of business and expect to win. It's vital that you adopt new playbooks that are designed to deliver more freedom, more fun and more flexibility. This book will give you the playbooks.

When the world changes, it produces winners and losers. This book is about giving you the new playbooks ahead of time so you can win.

What do you think of when you hear the word entrepreneur? Most people think of someone who raises money from a venture capitalist to create a groundbreaking new technology or disruptive business model. Elon Musk comes to mind first for many people globally – a man who in one month in 2024 launched a 23-storey rocket into space then had it fall back to earth and reverse parallel park into a giant pair of chopsticks; then he launched a humanoid robot prototype – a way of syncing your brain with a computer – and a campaign for free speech, a new fleet of vehicles and a new government department. By that standard, most people wouldn't dare to even aspire to be an entrepreneur.

What if the definition of an entrepreneur was a lot more gentle. What if being an entrepreneur simply meant that you are taking a personal risk, to build something commercially successful using resources that are currently outside of your control. This doesn't have to be a wildly disruptive new approach that turns an industry on its head; this could be a health or fitness clinic, a consulting firm, an IT service provider, a wedding planning service or a business that helps people with their pets.

The scale of your business might be relatively small. Someone like Elon Musk might not even recognize it as a proper business, but that doesn't matter. His businesses bring him endless stress at an unimaginable scale; your business might bring you new levels of enjoyment – who's the real genius? Your business might support wider goals like time with family, maintaining your health, travelling the world or volunteering for a charity. There's no rule that says a business has to raise money or create a new technology that disrupts anything at all. A business can be set up to deliver a wonderful lifestyle to the people who own and run it.

It is commonplace for entrepreneurs to get absolutely screwed over by venture capitalists. There are entrepreneurs who have built businesses worth over $500 million who did not earn anything significant from their venture because of the way the finance was structured with their venture backers. Many founders you have read about in the news whose companies achieved dizzying valuations and even big exits earned less than $5 million from the deal; they might have been better off buying a small agency, growing it and selling it. These people took on massive amounts of stress and focused their entire life on one thing for 5–10 years only to miss their targets and get cut out of the deal.

Famously, Hollywood star Jessica Alba was instrumental in the creation of the eco-friendly household goods business The Honest Company. When the business floated on the Nasdaq it was valued at a fantastic $1.7 billion and on paper Alba's stake was worth over $100 million. Unfortunately, her shares were locked up by her investors until even loftier targets had been achieved. Alba was able to take $3.5 million off the table but the rest of her shares are still in a contractual vault and she has stepped down from her role in the company. For a woman who can earn over $2 million per film she stars in, she might have been better off doing a deal with Netflix and saving herself the hassle.

Contrast this story with my own. I am an entrepreneur who owns a small group of businesses that I run with a group of close friends. At the time of writing, my businesses collectively have 8-figure revenues and employ about 100 people full-time. My businesses are profitable, I do not have investors who can control my decisions and I can live and work the way I want to. I have successfully sold businesses too, and when that has happened the money goes to my friends and me straightaway – there is no one standing in line before us stopping the flow of money until they get a 500% return first (as is possible with venture capital or private equity-backed companies).

I've worked hard to get into this position and it's taken me over 20 years to figure things out. I've endured chronic stress and lost relationships over poor business decisions. I spent over five years creating a business that was flawed by design. I've had the opposite of a lifestyle business – a business that was fuelled by enormous sacrifice and gave little back. I've ruined a lifestyle that was wildly fun and profitable by growing it bigger and making it too complex. This book is designed to share with you painful lessons I fought hard to learn so you don't have to make the same mistakes.

I now have multiple businesses including software, agencies and training. To be fair, my group of businesses are overkill when it comes to being a lifestyle entrepreneur. I could live very comfortably with any one of the businesses I own. Your life could be amazing with one business and a small team of 4–12 people. Knowing what I now know, I would recommend most people focus on achieving this goal to avoid overcomplicating things.

Based on my experience of building multiple businesses and working with over 5,000 entrepreneurs to create successful ventures of their own, I have constructed this book in two parts:

- **Part I: The seven mindset shifts that unlock your ability to create a lifestyle business.** Having a lifestyle business starts with a new way of seeing the world. The first half of this book covers the old way the world worked and contrasts it with the shifts that have created the new way. If it wasn't for these shifts, your lifestyle business wouldn't exist, so you need to be aware of them and how to approach the new world we are in.
- **Part II: The six business playbooks to move you from having an entrepreneurial idea to a fully developed lifestyle business.** These playbooks assume you are starting out from scratch in a new world of work and life. You'll start with an apprenticeship, then you'll conduct some experiments to build your confidence and, if you're ready, you'll build a small dynamic team to collaborate with.

When you read this book, you'll see a specific set of rules and steps to take. It might seem like it's rigid and narrow. You might think of plenty of examples that break the rules or deviate from the steps prescribed. This book is designed to outline a path that I know has a high chance of success for the times we are in. Are there other types of businesses that work? Of course. Can you be a 'solopreneur' with a great life – sure, there are people who have that figured out. Can you build an amazing business in a local geography? I'm sure plenty of people are doing that. Do some lifestyle businesses thrive without building the personal brand of the founder? Of course you can find them if you look.

This book steers you towards ideas that work best most of the time. In the same way, you can find people who survive a car crash without wearing a seatbelt, you can find successful pop-songs that go for over seven minutes, you can find some players in the NBA who are under 6 ft and there are examples of people who lose weight while eating donuts every day. Even though you can find examples of people who break the rules it doesn't mean rules aren't incredibly useful to follow. If you do find yourself breaking the rules, at least you know you're doing it deliberately. The rules aren't there to limit you, they are there to assist you and steer you towards choices that make your success easier more often than not.

In reading this book, I hope your mindset starts to shift so you can recognize amazing opportunities surrounding you right now. I hope you gain deeper clarity about the

business success available to you and how to get it. I want
you to avoid mistakes I have made, learn from my lessons
without having to endure the years of frustration and have a
step-by-step guide for going after a business that will make
your life magnificent.

Something to be clear about

You have come to this book for a reason. Most people
reading this will want specific steps to follow and you will
get them in these pages. It won't be enough though. Every
entrepreneur needs to bring something to the table that is
truly unique to them.

Your job is to discover your magic and then combine it
with the steps you find in books. Without this magic, the
steps won't work. Entrepreneurs can't be told everything –
being an entrepreneur is about unleashing something that is
personal to you into the world.

Enjoy reading the playbooks but stay tuned into your
own vision, mission and values. To get the most out of this
book, you will have to put these things in.

PART I

THE SHIFTS

CHAPTER 1

SHIFT 1: FROM INDUSTRIAL TO DIGITAL

Mindset shift: Understanding that the Industrial Revolution system has ended and is being replaced by the digital world we now live in. The rules of this system are different to the ones you were trained in and you must play by the new set of rules if you want to succeed.

In October 1806, Napoleon stood on a grassy battlefield of Jena facing the Prussian Army. He was outnumbered almost two to one. Napoleon's troops numbered 66,000 and Prince Hohenlohe of Prussia had mobilized 119,000 men for battle who had been preparing for this moment for a month.

On paper this should have been the end of the road for Napoleon – his troops were outnumbered and entering unfamiliar territory being defended by a proud and established military force. However, things did not go well for the defending Prussian army that day.

The Prussian army may have looked menacing from a distance but they were masking a fatal weakness. Their men were led by hereditary aristocrats who were disorganized, disobedient and unskilled. The Prussian army's ranks were based on a system of nepotism and flattery known as the Feudal System. The top roles had nothing to do with skill or merit and everything to do with birthright, virtue signalling and social games. The troops may have looked like one army but each regiment was loyal to their own feudal structure instead of a unified national identity. When orders were given from the so-called top, they had to be agreed to and re-given down the line through a discombobulated and unclear coalition of leaders who each had their own agenda in mind.

The Prussians were fidgeting that morning – rubbing their hands together to keep warm, they cast their eyes around wondering how each of their fellow soldiers would react when battle began. The French Army stood steely eyed – they were organized and followed a strict chain of command. When given orders, they didn't hesitate, they were ready to play their part in the expansion of the growing French Empire. Their ranks, led by the most skilled and experienced personnel, had been drilled into good form and motivated compliance.

As the sounds of muscats and cannons began to pop, the differences became painfully clear with the well-trained French army overwhelming the disjointed, disobedient and defective Prussians. At the end of the day, Napoleon had subjugated the Prussian King and was on his way to Berlin as their new Emperor to sign treaties that would embarrass and impoverish the defeated nation.

A decade later, the German-speaking regions had taken heed of their losses and constructed a plan to ensure they would never submit to such a cruel defeat ever again. They would establish a strong national identity and begin military training early; every child would attend a compulsory school system that would turn them from free-thinking, spirited children into compliant and obedient servants of the state. By the time they were teens, they would be ready to become loyal soldiers who would willingly fight, and die, for their country (the nation we now know as Germany).

The Prussian school system dressed children in uniforms and sat them in rows resembling the rank and file of a military parade. It introduced standardized testing, strict regimented days and a culture of blind obedience to authority. It wasn't optional – parents had to send their kids to school or risk being imprisoned; a clear message that the nation state was more powerful than the family unit.

By the mid-1800s, this structured, state-controlled, mandatory schooling system caught the eye of another group of people further afield. In 1843, Horace Mann, a Senator of Massachusetts, visited Germany in his capacity on the newly formed Board of Education. The Board of Education needed to solve a big problem unfolding in the USA.

As Horace Mann inspected classrooms in Prussia, his eyes lit up – he had found what he was looking for. His interest was not military but it was similar. He wanted to prepare children for factory work. The USA was rapidly industrializing and the factory owners were struggling to find adequate labour. Mann needed a way of manufacturing the American workers who would propel American manufacturing. What he encountered was vastly different from the disjointed, locally organized schools in the USA. He saw buildings laid out like army barracks, children separated by age and ability, dressed in uniform, answering questions correctly on command.

US children at the time were mostly schooled by Dames and church groups. They were given basic preparations before joining a family trade or helping on a farm but they weren't obedient and compliant when it came to the drudgery, danger and denigration of factory work. People didn't want to work this way; they wanted the variety, autonomy and more mellifluous pace of small business and farming. America was a land of migrants who had travelled from distant shores for freedom and opportunity; they hadn't come this far to staff a noisy, dangerous and dull factory. Horace Mann had found his answer – the compulsory Prussian school system could break the spirits of children early and prepare them for a life of servitude within the confines of a factory, industrial plant or mine. If he could achieve this at scale, the industrialists would have a steady stream of workers and the country would rapidly develop.

Soon after, in Britain, Robert Lowe passed laws to establish the compulsory school system, standardized testing and strict adherence to rules. Lowe was careful not to upset the British class system and he pioneered three schooling systems that would be acceptable to the elite.

For most children, the compulsory state system would prepare them for factory life, for upper-middle-class children Grammar schools would continue with a more classical education including subjects like Latin and Greek philosophy to prepare them for a life in the professions. The children of the wealthy and elite aristocracy would have exclusive schools that would focus on producing the ruling political class, of which Eton stands supreme to this day. For his extraordinary contribution to the industrialists in Britain, Lowe was raised to the peerage – he was made a viscount.

AGRICULTURAL INDUSTRIAL DIGITAL

AGRICULTURAL INDUSTRIAL DIGITAL

A new playbook had been created. This playbook was designed for the factory not the farm. It was a playbook that could scale up with the industrialized economy. The playbook for the Agricultural Age needed people to tend the land and produce food. It needed people who could work outdoors with their hands in exchange for their subsistence needs. The Feudal System had been a viable option for the Agricultural Age but it was breaking down when nations discovered the power of industry. The new playbook would be about turning humans into standardized parts that could fit into a factory and deliver economic prosperity.

As each nation industrialized, the compulsory schooling system we all know today developed alongside the factories and institutions. By the 1900s, a social contract emerged whereby we accepted this system in exchange for a few key perks – affordable housing, an eight-hour workday, a weekend, welfare programmes and a retirement age. In exchange for giving up our human spirit we would get safety, security and structure for life. At its apex, this system wasn't all that bad. A man could go to work in a factory and his wage could support a whole family of five. A woman raised children and made their family home into a place of love and connection. On one wage, they could afford hobbies, take road trips and indulge in the endless output that was flooding into consumer markets. He would work for one company most of his life and receive better and better pay and benefits each year; he would get more and more respect with regular promotions. She would be respected and adored for her role in raising the next generation.

The greatest benefit of all was the ability to become owners in the economy. By age fifty, if you followed this 'component labour playbook', the family home was paid off, savings had accumulated and a pension plan was ready to pay out. The family would marry off their daughters and send their sons to work in the factory. Then one day the man would be sent home for the last time to enjoy a decade of retirement before passing away. Work wasn't glamorous but this system had its perks.

This Industrial Revolution model was so successful that it lifted the majority of the world's population out of poverty. In 1900, almost 90% of the world's population was living in abject poverty and life expectancy was 35–40 years old in most parts of the world. By trading our free spirit and autonomy, humanity had achieved the dream of health and abundance. By the year 2000, over 80% of the world's population was no longer in abject poverty and it became normal for people to live past 70.

By the late 1900s, the abundant industrialized capitalist model gave birth to twins who would disrupt the component labour playbook. The first was abundant capital. The capitalist system invented finance; the ability to magic money from thin air and mobilize resources at speed today rather than having to wait. The second was digital technology, which could rapidly replace the jobs in factories and even in the professions. The impact of these two forces made the component labour playbook redundant. Abundant capital made homes too expensive to own and technology reduced the value of labour to the point that a household required two full-time workers just to live in a small flat in a city where the last remaining good jobs were. As a result, birth rates plummeted and home ownership became unattainable.

The component labour playbook has broken down on all fronts. There are no careers – if you stay at one company for too long you are more likely to be made redundant than receive a promotion. The eight-hour workday has been replaced by an always-on culture of endless emails and notifications that never sleep. A family home is unaffordable even for couples with both partners bringing home a full-time wage. Completing school isn't enough to get a decent job – a person needs a university degree too and that lands them in significant debt. As a couple hit age 40, they are lucky to be buying their first home and it's hardly a suitable dwelling to raise a family. Many professional couples in big cities live in tiny flats and terraced homes that would have historically been considered starter homes for unskilled labourers. This couple are under pressure just to stay married as each of them is changing jobs every few years. Their savings don't accumulate for long. Governments have become so large and indebted that record levels of tax burden is firmly on the shoulders of the middle class. Many couples who follow the rules of society choose not to have children or they delay and delay starting a family to the extent that it's more common than ever for a couple to have one or two kids and very rare to see three or four. When it comes time to retire, the government is finding ways to shirk all responsibility – pushing up the retirement age, reducing benefits, deflating the value of their currency and removing benefits.

Few publicly acknowledge that the industrial system has run its course. It's come to an end and we are left with a set of rules and paradigms that do not fit with the reality we are living in.

The schooling system prepared us to slot into a world that no longer exists. We are a product that has been churned out of a factory without a viable market to go into – we are the left-over stock from a campaign that ended last season. The schooling system was designed to produce obedient, functional component labour to work in any business or institution in the local area. That system still hasn't adapted to the world we live in now.

The world that has emerged is digitally powered, fuelled with abundant capital. This world does not need so many replaceable humans who follow orders blindly, doing repetitive, tedious work. We have computers, software, robots and artificial intelligence that can do most of it. What little factory work remains has been centralized in low-cost labour countries at a price far below what we can compete with in post-industrialized economies. Even white-collar work such as customer support, administration, programming, graphic design, legal compliance, accounting, video editing, marketing and employee management are being moved to places like Brazil, Africa, India, Thailand and the Philippines. If it's repetitive and it requires little more than a computer and a screen it's moving to a lower-cost country.

You were trained to function in a world that no longer needs your component labour. The unwritten social contract you were promised has been ripped up without your consultation and all the outcomes you were promised have been shipped somewhere else. For many people this realization will sting. It's unfair, there is a loss attached to this shift. You might want to fight it, you might want things to go back the way they were and you might argue the system was better the way it was. I get it and understand it – I came of age in the 1990s and experienced how great life was before digital technology disrupted everything. I have come to peace with the fact I can't change the ocean or the tides, all I can do is learn to surf the waves I'm on. The good news is that there is boundless opportunity now to have a magical life if you learn to manoeuvre through these trends successfully.

A new playbook is available, the one that is already being used by entrepreneurs all over the world. The new playbook leverages abundant technology and capital to produce a life that is worth living. This new playbook will allow you to live and work from anywhere. It will give you enough money to live in a big family home, raise children, travel in style and explore your passions and interests. Better yet, it won't require two people to work their guts out – most of the work will be done by technology and capital. If a couple wants to, they can adopt the traditional model of one income earner and one home maker. Alternatively, both could work part-time in one business or they could each have a business that follows the new playbook. The new playbook is even better than the component labour playbook was on its best day.

It is going to feel weird to adopt this new playbook because it feels almost forbidden. If you attended the traditional schooling system and have been part of Western culture for the last couple of decades it will feel strange to talk about having a great lifestyle and a wonderful home without even two people.

In the Agricultural Age humans organized themselves using a playbook called 'the Feudal System'. To become wealthy, you had to be endowed with fertile lands that you could protect. If you did not have lands, your time and effort went into extracting value from land for those who did. You were given subsistence food supplies in exchange for harvesting, preparing and moving food around.

Then industrial technology changed things. The invention of engines, electricity, fossil fuels and machinery removed most people from farming the land and freed them up to work in factories. The Industrial Age playbook replaced the Feudal System playbook. Vast amounts of land became less important. The wealthy were those who had the capital to set up a factory with machines, materials and workers. If you didn't have those things, you were given a job in the factory and in exchange for your compliance, you were allocated wages that enabled you to afford a home you could own and a short period of retirement. You had to sell your time and skills for money to those who had the leverage of capital.

The industrial system gave birth to finance and digital technology, which has created a completely new globalized world. In this new economy the physical factory has become less important. Wealthy people leverage intellectual property, media, data and software to build fortunes at the speed of light. If you play by the old rules in this new system you will fail. You must adopt a new playbook that allows you to turn your ideas into digital assets that deliver value at scale without you having to directly sell your time for money.

In this new digital economy, it is those who design and create intangible assets that win. These new assets scale at the speed of light, deliver value regardless of geography and replicate at zero marginal cost. The world is fast changing and so must you. These technologies will either drastically disrupt your way of life or dramatically improve it.

Ali Abdaal is an incredibly smart young man. He scored in the top of his class at Cambridge University studying medicine. Much to the delight of his family, he graduated and became a doctor within the National Health Service of the UK in 2018. He's also incredibly generous. As he was working as a doctor, he was also sharing his journey on YouTube. Despite 15-hour days in the hospital he found time to shoot and edit videos to help people with their lives.

These videos gained traction and he eventually attracted millions of views.

Ali is also very brave. In 2020, he made the wildly unpopular decision to quit medicine and become a YouTuber. This move was unthinkable at the time, to trade in the years of study to become a doctor to pursue podcasting and video-making for free wasn't something anyone expected. Ali recognized something important, the world was changing. Many of the older doctors he worked with weren't happy or even rich. Ali saw an alternative life path he could move to.

Today Ali Abdaal has millions of subscribers on YouTube, a ridiculously profitable business and a life of fun, freedom and fulfilment. Ali has a lifestyle business and he is able to improve even more lives each year than a doctor could hope to in an entire career. You have the same options available to you too. You can build a lifestyle business and you can impact people all over the world. You can experience more fun, freedom, fulfilment and financial success too.

The first shift you must make is to acknowledge that you were prepared for a world that no longer exists. Your education and training was designed to make you part of the machine but that machine is being replaced. Many of the ideas that were drilled into you are the opposite of what works today.

You were taught that you must face every test on your own. You were not encouraged to collaborate with the smartest people you knew in order to ace every exam – that was called cheating. In today's world, you will form relationships with collaborators who complement each other's strengths and weaknesses. You will ace every test together because as a team your chemistry is an asset that is worth more than any individual's skills. You are not a component that fits nicely into someone else's machine; you are a valuable part of a collective moving through the world together having adventures.

You were taught not to be an attention seeker. There came a day when you bound into the classroom full of life and energy, you told a joke and everyone cracked up laughing. You weren't praised for this, you were punished. The message was clear – don't stand out, don't be disruptive, just do your work. In today's world, not standing out is dangerous. One of the highest honours in the business world is to be described as a disruptor. The highest-paid people know how to be attention seekers – they burst into people's minds, they make jokes, they get a reaction and they make more money because they can do this.

You were taught not to use technology. You can't use a calculator to do your math test. You can't take your smartphone into your history exam. You certainly can't generate the answers with AI to graduate. In real life, if you're not using technology all the time to do as much as possible, then you are going to be left behind. There may have been a time when learning the basics without the help of technology was wise but you leave that lesson behind now.

You were taught that turning up on time at a particular place was supremely valuable. Being late or not showing up at all was one of the worst things you could do regardless of your grades. In today's world, you don't need to be anywhere in particular to create value, and if you can get a great result in 2 hours at 2 a.m., it's more valuable than doing average work for 8 hours between 9 a.m. and 5 p.m.

All of these things you learned, need to be unlearned. You have to get yourself comfortable with the idea that work can be fun. Your value is in your ability to make friends, cause a ruckus, copy the answers to the test from the smartest people you know, download the homework and do it all from wherever you want to be. You have to explore your mind and do a clean-out of the old ideas and replace them with the new ones that serve you better.

Activity:

Chart a timeline of your career to date. Identify the skills you learned at each stage of your journey. Identify stories that are unique to you and themes that stand out. Consider what you want to be known for going forward.

AI prompt:

'I want to prepare myself for the big changes that are coming in my industry. In particular, AI is going to disrupt the way I work and will create new opportunities for me to explore. Ask me questions to discover how I can adapt and prepare to make the most of the next five years.'

CHAPTER 2

SHIFT 2: FROM MASS MARKET TO NICHES

> **Mindset shift: Seeing that the mass market will not deliver the right customers for your business and recognizing affluent niche markets contain your ideal customers.**

'Why do we cheat? And why do happy people cheat? And when we say "infidelity", what exactly do we mean? And is an affair always the end of a relationship?'

Standing in front of a room full of the world's richest and most powerful people, couples therapist Esther Perel has been on stage less than a minute and already she has commanded their full attention. You can hear a pin drop – in a room of elite individuals with unlimited lifestyle options, every single person has been effected by the questions she is asking. Either they have thought about cheating, they have cheated, their partner has had an affair or someone very close to them has.

It's a particularly hot topic in these circles. When a couple has fame and fortune, an affair is publicly embarrassing and financially catastrophic. For any of the people in this room, just the thought of a divorce makes them wince as they tally up the legal costs, capital destruction and moments of public shame. Esther Perel knows this; she's had these conversations with these people many times in her decades as a couples therapist. It is her specialty.

When she talks about infidelity, she comes at it in a unique way that her wealthy clients resonate with. She empathizes with them and describes the conundrums they face. She uses words and phrases common to that set of people. She discusses ideas that very few therapists would understand if they only work with 'normal people'. Her book *Mating in Captivity* has struck a chord, especially with the elite end of town.

Esther Perel is a bestselling author and sought-after professional speaker. She's also the creator of a communication game and has a global network of couples therapists who are trained up in her methods. In this room, however, you'll find people who do not want to buy a book or a game; they want to know how they can work directly with her, no matter the cost. For people who have over $30 million of assets, a divorce would cost millions and therefore it would be no barrier to spend upwards of $250,000 on couples therapy if it prevented the breakdown of a marriage.

Most couples therapists do not charge anywhere close to that money and most couples wouldn't dream of spending it. A typical couples therapist, even in a wealthy city like New York or Sydney might cost $150–$300 per session. If you surveyed most couples on how much they would be willing to spend on couples therapy you would probably arrive at a number like $500–$1,500 per year. Couples therapy isn't typically known to be a licence to print money.

For Esther Perel, despite her fees being astronomical, she has a waiting list. This is because she has figured out something important. Her value massively increases when she's talking to the right person.

Ask most couples therapists about their business and they will probably reveal their geography in the first few sentences. 'I have a private practice based in Down Town Miami', they might say. Too bad if you don't live near there, that's where their business is. Ask Esther Perel about her business and she will not mention geography at all; she will tell you about the problems she solves, the solutions she offers and the types of people she serves – no matter where they are in the world.

Before the Digital Age, almost all businesses were limited by geography. It would be fair to say that prior to 2010, the location of a business would have matched very closely to the location of its customers. Naturally there were some exceptions and we gave them a special name – 'multinational corporations'. Until very recently, if you described a business as being a 'multinational' you must have been describing a

business with thousands of employees placed in tall buildings in cities across the globe. We would assume you were
talking about Coca-Cola, Nike or Deloitte.

That's no longer true. During the Covid-19 pandemic,
millions of businesses discovered that geography played
much less of a leading role in their business than they first
thought. Suddenly lawyers were consulting with their clients
on Zoom, entertainers were organizing live events with
people in multiple time zones, live conferences sprung
up without anyone booking a meeting room. We all got a
glimpse of a new reality where value could easily be delivered remotely at a fraction of the cost. Suddenly many small
businesses became 'multinational'.

In one fell swoop, the geographical limits of businesses
ceased to exist briefly and for a lot of people there was
no going back. Once you break free from the geographical
paradigm the world looks very different. Instead of building a business that meets the needs of your local community who share the same postcode, you can create an offer
that meets the needs of a community of people who share
the same problems or issues. It doesn't matter where these
people are – it only matters that you can connect with
them online.

Before the Covid-19 lockdowns, my business plan was
to open up offices in 20 cities. I imagined having entrepreneurs all over the world attending local workshops in
their city. Each city would have its own city team running
the business and local mentors leading the training programmes. By 2019, we had opened in eight cities and a huge

amount of my headspace went into thinking about how to run a business across so many locations.

When we were forced into lockdowns in 2020, we started running our training programmes on Zoom. We discovered that we could offer the workshops on three time zones and cover the entire planet. Suddenly it didn't matter where our clients were based or even where our team lived. This totally freed up our thinking to simply focus on the types of clients we served best and the problems they wanted to solve. It also freed us up to hire the team members with the best fit for our culture regardless of where they wanted to live.

When we were focused on solving the geographical problems, enormous amounts of money went into offices, boardrooms and event venues. As soon as we took the business online, we reallocated that money to more resources for our clients. We also went from offering one workshop a month to weekly workshops. The value our clients perceived went through the roof. They never cared about workshop venues; they cared about achieving outcomes as quickly and easily as possible.

If your business is based on a geography your costs go up and your prices are forced down. You price your services based upon the average person within a 10-mile radius instead of focusing on the value of solving the 10 biggest problems your perfect client wants solved. When you are geographically focused, you spend money on stuff your customers don't care so much about rather than innovating solutions that really matter to them. When your business is based on solving a problem for a distinct group of people, you focus your effort and price your offer based on what it's worth to those people.

Your successful lifestyle business will be based on something called 'ideal customer personas' or ICPs. An ICP is a way of describing the type of customer you are looking for. This description will typically characterize key things about your potential customer such as their typical situation, their frustrations, goals, inhibitors, budget and their mindset towards buying something. What you will want to avoid is pinning this ICP down to one location.

Based on the problem your business solves, your business has a total addressable market of people it could theoretically serve. These people could be anywhere in the world. The moment you deliberately limit your business to a geography you have made a decision that cuts you off from people who have a need you could one day address. You do not want to define your business by a geography because it's only a matter of time before a digital business, that can serve people anywhere in the world, will take your customers – but you won't be able to take theirs. If, however, your business focus is global from day one, you will reach out to people based on their needs not their location. You can even be hyper-focused in who you target based on their specific desires and there will still be many of them – 70% of the world's population has fast internet.

Esther Perel's ideal customer is an ultra-high net worth married couple. In Esther's hometown of Antwerp, Belgium, there might be a few hundred ultra-high net worth couples.

In New York, where Esther has lived for many years there are several thousand ultra-high net worth couples, if her business is limited to this geography. When Perel wrote a book and delivered talks that would be seen by millions of people globally, she opened herself up to the global market of ultra-high net worth couples – of which there are over 300,000 with over $40 trillion in assets.

Consider that Esther Perel only needs 10 high net worth clients per year for her to earn millions in counselling fees. By carefully crafting her message to resonate with an elite ICP, she has tipped the power dynamic so far in her favour that her clients will jump on a private jet to have a face-to-face therapy session.

What you offer has a different value in the eyes of different types of people. You must discover who has the most to gain from what you do. To a single man, couples therapy isn't worth anything. To happy newlyweds in the honeymoon phase of their marriage, couples therapy might be worth a few thousand dollars at most. To a billionaire whose divorce will make the news and destroy decades of work and sacrifice, couples therapy is worth almost any price.

Your ICP needs to be someone who has a problem or desire they want resolved; they also have money available to throw at the solution and you need to be able to communicate with them in a way that influences their behaviour. If you are targeting a customer who doesn't have money to throw at their problems, it's not the right target customer. If they don't have a strong desire to solve a problem or fulfil a desire, it's not the right target customer. If you are in no position to influence these people, it's not the right target customer.

Too often, entrepreneurs aim their offering at the middle of the market. In a digital, global world this is one of the worst mistakes. At the late stages of the Industrial Age, the middle of the market was affluent. School teachers, police officers, office managers, chefs, mechanics and journalists all made enough money to pay for a home, raise a family and buy the latest gadgets. That is rapidly going away – from 2010 to 2020 the number of UK school teachers who could afford to buy a home in the catchment area of their school halved from about 40% to 20%. The middle market is not a place you will find disposable income the way you once did decades ago.

Today, the money has moved to the top of the market. The top 1% of earners in the USA and the UK make about 15% of all the income. The next 9% make about 30% of the total income earned. This means the top 10% of earners have about 45% of the income and the bottom 90% of earners share about 55% of the total income. The numbers of people moving towards high incomes is on the rise too.

For your lifestyle business to thrive you will need to target the top 10% of earners in the developed world. These people are in two categories:

- **The luxury market:** This is the top 1% of earners who are cash rich and time poor. They like to save effort by buying the best of everything. They are not concerned with price but they do care a lot about pedigree, status and theoretical resale or investment value. If you look at the typical mass market price of any good, the luxury shopper will pay 30–100 times more for almost the same thing. A decent stainless steel mechanical watch on Amazon costs about $150, whereas a Rolex will set you back more than $10,000. The same can be said for almost any goods that have luxury versions, and this isn't limited to wine, watches, cars, fashion and hotels; you will find luxury nannies, consultants, security guards, dentists, fitness trainers and ghost writers too. Almost anything you can think of has a luxury version that oozes status, pedigree and investment value and sells for orders of magnitude more than the mass market offering.

- **The affluent niche market:** This is typically someone who is in the top 10% of earners and they are passionate about a topic to the extent that they join groups, buy books and follow influencers or gurus relating to this topic. When these people get into wine, fitness, mediation, psychedelics, leadership, art, philanthropy, technology or travel you know about it. They order a pile of books, watch YouTube videos, book tickets to conferences and commit to courses or coaches relating to this passion. They are not shopping on price, they are shopping on passion.

Outside of the luxury market or an affluent niche market, you'll find the mass market. The mass market typically shop on price first. They have a budget in mind and they compare their options to get the most bang for their buck. No matter how much passion, experience or pedigree your business can offer, you'll be judged against alternative options that are similar but cheaper. You will become demoralized as time after time you are forced to justify your prices as if that is all that matters. The mass market was once a vibrant place powered by a strong middle-class consumer but today it has become crowded, noisy with eroded spending power.

The mass market is a race to the bottom you want to avoid by skilfully campaigning to position yourself as a leading voice within the affluent niche market, maybe even the luxury end when your reputation grows.

Within your affluent niche market you will find your ICP. This describes exactly the person your business is focused on. You want to craft a detailed description of this person.

You want to know exactly what their problems are and how they describe them. You want to understand the specific outcomes they want to achieve and the precise images they imagine when they think about them. You want to know what they've previously tried that didn't work. You want to know the other brands they like, what their favourite books are, who they subscribe to on YouTube and anything else that completes the picture of who your offer is perfectly designed for. The more clear you can be, the easier it is to spot these people everywhere.

The starting point is to ask the powerful question: 'who sees the most value in what I offer?' Your value is entirely subjective. It varies wildly, depending on who's looking at you. If you can double the marketing results of a small consulting business, your fee could be justifiably $20,000. If you could double the marketing results for a large consulting business, your fee could justifiably be $1 million and the underlying method could be almost the same.

A client of mine, Ray Littlefield, began his career working in the manufacturing plant of Toyota and learned their iconic 'Lean Methodology' directly from some of the world's most respected practitioners. He was able to set up a consultancy teaching this approach to a wide variety of businesses. After several years training and certifying lean practitioners across 50 different types of businesses he asked the questions: 'Of all my clients, who sees the most value in what I do and can afford to pay it? Who has the most to gain from what I know? Who am I most passionate about working with?'

Researching and pondering the answers to these questions led him to his affluent niche market. He discovered that his best clients were family businesses that had been manufacturing something for more than 30 years. The businesses were in the hands of the second or third generation. Their manufacturing plant was becoming outdated, the founder of the business had retired or passed away and the thought of transforming the facility was daunting to say the least. Hundreds of jobs were at stake, millions of dollars needed to be invested and mistakes could be catastrophic.

This was Ray's favourite type of client to serve and this type of client viewed Ray and his team as a godsend. Ray has successfully positioned himself as a 'key person of influence' in the eyes of these multi-generational, family-run manufacturing businesses. His consulting firm, Niwaki, does not need to run expensive marketing campaigns, nor does it need to compete on price. Their reputation precedes them and their niche market is happy to pay for the added value, nuanced experience and dedicated passion Niwaki can bring.

Once you can clearly identify an ICP within an affluent niche, your next challenge is to influence their behaviour. To do this, you must demonstrate that you are a key person of influence within their topic of interest. Your name needs to come up in conversations and your face needs to show up in their social media feed. When they research you, they must feel a sense of excitement to have found someone who's as passionate and dedicated as they are. Your personal brand as a key person of influence is far more powerful than a purely business brand. A business brand is fine if you want to compete on price in the mass market but it's lousy at communicating passion.

Ray Littlefield isn't well known in broad circles but if he attends a conference on lean manufacturing for mid-sized family run businesses he's a rock star. He will be one of the speakers on the stage and at break times he will have a circle of people around him asking questions. People will ask him for his contact details and feel thrilled to get his personal e-mail. When he leaves the conference, he goes back to being a normal person – he's not famous for the mass market despite being revered in his industry.

Your lifestyle business will exist within a community of people who value your passion, your commitment to experience and your thought leadership over and above a short-term saving from a cheap supplier. Resist the desire to please everyone or even be understood by everyone. To a small group of people you will offer something they love and are willing to pay for. Outside of that group, it doesn't matter what people think.

Activity:

Go to the fanciest hotel or restaurant in your area and ask yourself the question: 'If I only worked one day per month, who would pay the most amount of money for a day of my time – what would I have to offer for them to pay me a month's income in a day?' Consider the types of problems you solve. Consider the return on investment someone could get if they followed your advice. Look around the room at some of the people, imagine what they might do for work or business and imagine how you might improve their life in a meaningful way. Now imagine you are invited as a guest speaker at a very niche conference full of passionate people who can't wait to see your presentation. Who are the types of people at this conference and what do they want to see from you? Journal your ideas and take note of the types of people who see the most value in what you do.

AI prompt:

'I want to create an ideal customer persona avatar for my business. My ICP will be someone who sees enormous value in what I have to offer, they will have available budget to spend with me and I will be able to solve a meaningful problem for them. My story and unique experiences will be of particular interest to them and will signal to my ICP that I have something they want. Ask me questions about the value I have and then create a detailed description of the ICP who would see the most value in what I can offer.'

CHAPTER 3

SHIFT 3: FROM TIME AND SKILLS TO CONTENT AND CODE

> **Mindset shift: Moving beyond the value of your time and skills to produce valuable intellectual property, media, data and technology.**

As you scroll through videos on your phone, a young man in his early twenties excitedly shouts 'Over the house football throw!' then spikes a ball high up over the roof of a two-storey home. He dashes through the front door, runs through wrapping paper, knocks over a table full of people eating, runs up a set of stairs chased by a teddy bear, he pops a dozen balloons, fights off a group of sumo wrestlers, knocks over a hundred toilet rolls, runs through a gym where a gorilla is boxing a dinosaur and then runs into the backyard to tackle an alien out of his way as he catches the football as it descends from over the roof. The young man screams 'Subscribe!'

The whole thing takes 35 seconds. It seems silly, playful and pointless until you realize that behind the scenes this is driving a seriously successful business.

The young man is a YouTuber named Jesse Riedel, known more widely by his YouTube channel name 'Jesser'. This short video has been watched over 200 million times and Jesse has well over 23 million subscribers on his YouTube channel. Jesser makes these short videos every week, also longer videos about basketball and playing pranks with his friends. He also has an apparel company called Bucketsquad, selling basketball clothing featuring his unique designs at a premium price. On top of that, he has a dozen companies sponsoring his social media accounts to reach his audience. He even gets paid to go to sports games around the world.

The small team at Jesser are making millions in profit each year doing something fun. They have flexibility to work the way they want to work and they have the freedom to turn their ideas into new business opportunities whenever they want. Jesser has set up a huge basketball court they film on, he owns the house he does pranks in and he and his team are often found working on their laptops and phones in cafes and airport lounges. He's focused on a relatively affluent niche – 'Gen Z basketball bros'. He's created a products and media just for his followers while ignoring the wider market of sports fans of all ages.

The schooling system taught Jesse Riedel that the way to be valuable was through his time and skills. Like millions of kids, he was told to sit down, pay attention, learn the curriculum and become a boring, repeatable person if he wanted to succeed. School did not like him being a class clown and capturing attention. School told him that he wasn't going to make it unless he could calm down and stop being so disruptive. As it turns out the opposite is true. The kids in Jesse's school who followed the plan can't get jobs, can't buy houses and can't earn enough to live comfortably in a big city. Jesser, on the other hand, is making millions doing what he loves.

You probably feel uncomfortable with the idea of making money by throwing a football over your roof and running through your house like a mad person. You learned that your value had to be linked to something serious like practising law or medicine. You learned that making money was all about turning up to work on time every day and doing things in a careful and strategic way. Making money wasn't meant to be fun or exciting – it's the by-product of effort and consistency over time. Right?

There is a universal rule about making money, which is that your ability to earn is based on your ability to add value at scale.

$$\text{value} \times \text{scale} = \text{earning power}$$

During the Industrial Age, there was only one way for most people to be more valuable. Through education you moved from unskilled to skilled labour. If you were highly educated, you could offer highly skilled labour. The way that you could add value at scale was through a large corporation. The bigger the business you worked for, the greater the scale. The aim for many ambitious people in the Industrial Age was to become highly skilled (value) and work for a large multinational brand (scale).

In the Digital Age, you have more options. You now have direct access to scale through online platforms. You are also in a position to create new forms of value that are not directly linked to selling your time and skills for money.

To build a lifestyle business, you must understand the full range of options you have to deliver value at scale. The 'value hierarchy' is a useful way of thinking about your choices.

At the bottom of the value leverage hierarchy is unskilled component labour. This is the starting point for young adults. They have time and energy but are unskilled in how to deploy this resource. As a 14-year-old, I got my first job at McDonald's. On day one, I arrived full of excitement but completely unable to do anything helpful. The first training we received was a step-by-step lesson on how to sneeze correctly. 'I want you to know two things – we are working with food and we have a system for everything at McDonald's. Including sneezing', we were told.

It was a wonderful experience to be trained up on how to run a restaurant. In my first year, I was able to run the kitchen area during a lunch rush and produce thousands of dollars' worth of fast food per hour. McDonald's are masters in turning unskilled teenagers into productive employees.

Learning skills and gaining experience takes us up a level on the value hierarchy to skilled labour. The schooling system is built to create component labour. University and work experience then turns unskilled labour into skilled labour. Once you have the skills, you were told you can then enjoy job security. Not any more – in essence it's a trap that locks you into selling your time for money to either one employer or to multiple clients through self-employment. The problem with being skilled labour is you are only earning money when you are working.

In a fast-moving world, this trap compounds when you consider the time it takes to win work. In the Industrial Age, people often worked for just a few employers in their whole career but in today's economy people are changing jobs every few years and contractors, consultants or agencies might need to win a new client every month. This treadmill of endlessly winning work then delivering work is exhausting – and it gets even worse.

If you work predominantly on a screen, the internet has put every skilled individual in competition with every other skilled person on the planet. It's not enough to be the best architect in Manchester, you are going to be compared with architects in Munich, Mumbai and Manhattan before you win a new client.

The way out of this trap is to move to the higher levels of the value hierarchy. Above skilled labour is intellectual property (IP) and it's the key to creating your freedom with a lifestyle business.

Intellectual property is rooted in your know-how, expertise, stories, insights and reputation. As you have lived your life you have gathered this potential intellectual property and it's sitting below the surface waiting for you to formalize it.

I spent the first 10 years of my career making normal people famous in new markets. I ran a marketing business called Triumphant Events, specializing in promoting and running workshops, roadshows and demo days for new products. I worked with several founders and chief executive officers (CEOs) to put them in front of thousands of people each month at live events to scale their businesses. I was running over a hundred events per year in Australia and the UK, managing complex marketing campaigns, crafting pitches, directing my clients on how to build their personal brands so that more people would show up to events.

In 2009, my business was almost wiped out due to the global financial crisis. My two main clients couldn't afford to work with us. I had to let 90% of my team go. My bank balance evaporated. In 2008, I was regularly running events with thousands of people, making millions in sales and getting paid to tour the world. In 2009, I moved from a penthouse apartment into my sister's spare room, I ran some events with 30–50 people and I injured myself twice so badly I could barely move. Almost everything I had worked for in the preceding decade was gone. Life was trying to slow me down so I could see something.

I spent a lot of time that year trying to figure out my next moves, What was I good at? What insights did I possess that others found interesting? What valuable knowledge had I accumulated? What stories did people want me to share? Who did I have in my network? What resources could I still leverage? I started getting clarity – I knew how to make CEOs famous and get them ready for the stage; I knew how to promote events and get thousands of people to show up; I was friends with amazing professional speakers and I had a trusted reputation even though I'd fallen off my perch (in fairness a lot of people were in the same position that year).

At the end of 2009, I decided to go for broke. I would use all the remaining resources I had left to run a big event called 'Make It Big 2010'. I spent £10,000 booking a celebrity business speaker and begged a mentor figure to launch his book at my event. If it failed, at least I would go out on a bang. In the lead-up to the event, amid the fear and frantic planning, I started to write about the power of building a personal brand as a founder or CEO.

With a razor-thin budget and a stretched team of just three people, I hosted a two-day event for over

900 entrepreneurs. Our message of hopeful optimism hit the mark and the selection of speakers drew in the crowd. When I took the stage as a speaker, it was the first time people saw me sharing my own ideas. I talked them through my insights on how the world was changing due to the financial crisis, what I had learned from the 'Obama 08' social media campaign and my method for becoming a key person of influence.

It was a hit! Forty people in the audience enrolled onto the first 'Key Person of Influence Accelerator' and another dozen joined the waiting list for the second cohort. The dark clouds lifted and I was suddenly hopeful again and I was back in business.

The following year I formalized my ideas into a set of books, frameworks, videos, online portals, brand assets and registered intellectual property. I then raised £400,000 for 10% of the business. Discovering and developing my own IP allowed me to go from having a business based on my skilled labour to having something scalable, worth millions, in just 18 months. I went from working 70-hour weeks with a handful of clients to being able to develop hundreds of entrepreneurs every year working half the time.

So how do you create your own intellectual property? You must commit to regularly pause, reflect and document. Pausing, reflecting and documenting is the process of discovering the goldmine that sits inside your story.

In the last 24 months, you probably did something special that got an interesting outcome. Maybe you had a post that went viral on social media, maybe you solved a complex problem for a client, maybe you ran a well-received event or delivered an important outcome ahead of time and budget. You must pause, reflect on the story and document the key attributes. Those are seeds of valuable IP you are discovering.

There is a magic question to help you find your valuable IP. The magic question is: 'When did I do something special, for a certain type of person, where we got a valuable result and I can explain it step by step?'

This question contains all the elements of saleable and valuable IP. Doing 'something special' implies that it was unique, it wasn't commonplace. Doing this for 'a certain type of person' points to the potential for a wider market of people who will be interested in this. The fact that you got a 'valuable result' means you can charge money to deliver that result to others. And if you can 'explain it step by step' then you have a methodology that can be leveraged to deliver value at scale.

Pause, reflect and document: Taking time in silence doesn't feel like work but it can be some of the highest paid work there is.

On a weekly basis you should carve out time to pause, reflect on this magic question and document the examples that come up. If you are already in business, you potentially have hundreds of examples to choose from. Every happy client is an example. The way you work with your suppliers, the way you win business or the way you approached an important deal all contains the potential for IP.

The more you document, the more you will start to notice the themes to what you do. Suddenly it all clicks and you realize that you have something valuable that could scale much greater than selling time for money. Capturing your intellectual property is a key ingredient for creating your lifestyle business.

When you are familiar with the magic question and you understand how to spot intellectual property you will start to see it everywhere, especially when you look at some of the super successful entrepreneurs who have a lifestyle business. Simon Sinek was a consultant facilitating workshops for growth companies. One day he paused, reflected and documented unique intellectual property to help businesses to 'Start With Why' and discover their deeper purpose, create a potent culture and grow faster. Chris Voss paused, reflected and documented his lessons from being an FBI hostage negotiator, wrote the book *Never Split the Difference* and started a scalable negotiation school for businesses all over the world to learn from. Codie Sanchez paused, reflected and documented her experiences of buying boring businesses like laundromats and car washes and wrote *Main Street Millionaire*, which is now helping thousands of business-minded people to acquire a company.

Discovering your valuable intellectual property leads perfectly into the next level of the value hierarchy, which is media.

Media is anything people can watch, read or listen to online. Books, videos, podcasts, photos, blogs, reports, diagrams, documentaries and magazines are all examples of media assets. Not long ago, these assets were expensive to produce and distribute. Only big companies could invest in media assets when I was starting out in business.

Not now – teenagers armed with nothing more than a basic smartphone create all of these assets and share them with the world effortlessly.

The best media assets that deliver the most value are ones built on your IP. When you have done something special with a certain type of person, capture the story on video and put it on YouTube. When you have discovered a step-by-step approach to delivering a valuable outcome, turn it into a report and make it available for download. If you've reflected on the value of the results you can reliably get for people, share those reflections on a podcast episode.

These assets drive your lifestyle business. Your lifestyle business will have thousands of people watching your content every week. You will be featured on podcasts that will drive your lifestyle business forward. Your website will have special downloads; your social media profiles will regularly share images and updates. Without leaving your front door, thousands of people from all over the world will have a positive experience of you and your business each week. These media assets will set you free from the trap of using your time to win business – new clients will discover you through your media assets.

When people see your media assets, they will want more. They will want to make sure they don't lose you in the noise. They want access to more of your intellectual property and more of your interesting media. To be sure they don't miss out, they will share with you their data. Data is the next form of value you can leverage, completely separate from your time.

Data is primarily the people you can contact and your ability to know what they want. If you have a list of names and e-mails on a spreadsheet, you have a data asset. If you have followers on your Instagram account or subscribers on YouTube, that could be considered a data asset too. The key is to own and enrich your data. You want to know as much as possible about each person who's interacting with your lifestyle business and you want that data on your own systems.

You ideally want people to fill in forms that tell you about them and give you permission to contact them on an ongoing basis. A powerful approach is to set up an online questionnaire, scorecard, quiz or assessment. When I created the 'Key Person of Influence Scorecard' in 2015, I had no idea it would be the key to doing over $20 million of new business in the following few years. Over 90,000 people completed the quiz and self-assessed their need to access my intellectual property on becoming a key person of influence.

Note: It's quick and easy to set up an online assessment using ScoreApp.com

First I developed my own intellectual property, then I wrote the book (media) and then launched the scorecard to collect data. That winning combination generated thousands of valuable client relationships on autopilot because it was all held together with technology.

Technology is at the apex of the value hierarchy. Your ability to leverage through software and AI is key to having the ultimate lifestyle business but it is dependent on first having unique intellectual property, engaging media assets and access to a growing database of potential customers.

With IP, media and data, your software and AI systems can come to life and start delivering value at scale without you being aware of it.

Your lifestyle business will have a tech-stack of tools you rely on from other suppliers and eventually you will create your own proprietary software. Software was once out of reach for most businesses. Then it became more accessible through software subscriptions designed to be a good fit for a wide number of businesses. In a post-AI world, most businesses will be able to custom build software solutions totally unique to their needs. They will 'vibe-code' software into existence just by telling an AI what solution they are looking for. What once cost eye-watering amounts of money to create can be created in hours, almost for free today.

Your lifestyle business will also have autonomous AI agents doing most of the work. Most of your customer success team will be AI agents – likewise your IT developers, your bookkeeper, legal counsel and research team will also be AI agents. Your lifestyle business will have a small number of real people commanding an army of AI agents and software solutions that bring your IP, media and data to life.

The school system only revealed the base levels of the value hierarchy and hence most people are stuck selling their time and skills. In an economy built on digital assets that scale, time and skills aren't fit for purpose anymore. You must pause, reflect and document your IP. You must turn your IP into media. Then let your media attract rich data and let your software and AI systems turn all of it into an exciting business.

Activity:

Go for a walk in nature but do not take your phone or headphones. Instead take a notepad and pen. Before you set off, write at the top of a page 'when did I do something special, for a certain type of person, and we got a remarkable result and I can explain it step by step?' Head out for your walk and let your mind wander. Find yourself a bench and sit for a while with your thoughts, reflect on the question and write down examples. When you have more than three examples, notice if there are themes or trends to the special things you've done.

AI prompt:

'Ask me questions about my past five years to discover if I have anything of interest that could form the basis of valuable intellectual property or a book that people would want to read. When you spot any themes or trends state exactly what you notice. If you have suggestions for a book I should write, give me a book overview. If you already know something about me from previous interactions that would indicate valuable ideas or experiences, stories that could become intellectual property, make suggestions.'

CHAPTER 4

SHIFT 4: FROM MANUFACTURING SUPPLY TO MANUFACTURING DEMAND

> **Mindset shift: Seeing a business primarily as an engine for generating demand first and then delivering on what customers have signalled interest in second.**

When he's on the move, he's really on the move. In a Rolls Royce car, a Segway scooter or a private jet. Myron Golden had polio as an infant and as a result, one of his legs didn't develop as much strength or mass as normal. Throughout his whole life, he's had the support of a metal leg brace just to walk. That hasn't slowed him down. In his youth he became a black belt in karate and competed in tournament competitions. He started as an entrepreneur at age 25 and had about a 14-year learning curve before he ever earned a six-figure sum. However, now he spends a lot of his time driving around in his Rolls Royce, flying in a private jet or cruising along the coast of Florida in a power yacht. When he hosts a conference, he prefers to zip around on a two-wheel electric Segway; he effortlessly glides through the hotel foyer at a speed most people have to jog to keep up.

Myron invited me to speak at his signature event 'Offer Mastery Live' where he teaches entrepreneurs the ins and outs of offers. On this particular day, Myron is standing in front of a room of 600 people who are attending his event. Myron needs a security guard with him at all times. The audience love him so much that he gets mobbed whenever he goes anywhere – they all want to chase after him, get a photo with him and tell him how much impact he's had on their business and life. These people have read his books and followed him on social media for years, so seeing him in person is an electrifying experience. The security guard is there to make sure he can get in and out of the building without doing four hours of selfies each time.

Throughout the three-day conference Myron is not selling anything; he's delivering non-stop value. He's in his mid-60s with a significant disability but he gives off the energy of an athlete half that age. On the second day of the conference he takes questions from the audience and it becomes apparent that several people want to know how they can work with him personally. They love the books, videos and big events but they want some one-on-one time.

Myron senses the tension in the room. He has 600 people standing before him like a pride of hungry lions staring at a plump elk. They are hungry to buy, they want whatever he's got on offer – even though he hasn't mentioned a thing. Through his stories, frameworks and insights, he has shown them his value and they want as much as they can get. This isn't a surprise to Myron – he has crafted his presentation to deliver maximum value and he's banking on this moment arriving. He has carefully manufactured palpable desire in the room and he's about to channel it into a sales frenzy.

Myron says that he will not be making a sales pitch to this room because that's not what he had promised for this conference. Instead he tells the audience that for those of them that would like to hear his sales pitch, they can follow him to another room at the lunch break on the final day. He says that if you want to hear what he has to offer, you can request access to attend that separate room by filling in a detailed form about your business needs.

The following day, as lunchtime approaches, I am curious to see how many people have applied to attend his sales pitch rather than going off for lunch. When he announces the break and invites people to head to the other room I am shocked to see about 80% of the room get up and make their way to the alternative venue. Inside it's standing room only with Myron raised up on his two-wheel Segway as a stage. He delivers his pitch powerfully and divides the room into three categories. The first category could loosely be described as business owners who already have $100,000 to $1 million of revenue. The second category of entrepreneurs has a business with $1 million–$10 million of revenue and the final category already has a business with sales in the tens of millions. For each category, he has crafted a perfect offer that suits their needs. The pricing ranges from $25,000 to $1 million per year.

He makes them an offer and invites them to complete their sales forms. When the dust settles, over $6 million in sales forms have been handed in on the spot. Included in those sales forms are two people who have opted for the $350,000 offer, and one person who has opted for the highest value package – one-on-one coaching time with Myron for $1 million. But as amazing as that is, more than 135 people said yes to either a $27,000 offer or a $55,000 offer, both of which are one year of group coaching. In a saturated industry Myron is fully booked. And he has helped many of his clients model and match his success.

Entrepreneurship isn't fair. You don't get a fair day's pay for a fair day's work. You get paid by market forces.

The market doesn't care how hard you work, how much effort you put in, how passionate you are or how bad you want to succeed. It doesn't care that you've objectively 'earned it' or that you're more experienced or qualified than others.

There are thousands of business coaches who are just as good as Myron Golden when it comes to coaching clients but they don't make millions in a weekend because they aren't as skilled at manufacturing desire. They focus on the supply of high-quality coaching, not the demand for high-quality coaching.

Entrepreneurial success cares a lot about demand and supply. If you're good at generating demand for something in relatively short supply you have done something the market values. If you can deliver value at scale then you earn money relative to that value at that scale. Everything else is irrelevant to the market.

Imagine that there were such things as profit gods who hand out money fairly based on how much value a business delivers, how much risk it takes and how powerfully it can innovate. Surely the profit gods would reward airlines with massive margins. Airlines have to do everything right – safety, customer service, capital allocation, long-term planning, 24/7 complex logistics and adherence to global regulations. Why then does the average airline make an average profit margin of around 5%? There are no profit gods handing out profit fairly – it's purely demand and supply tension that dictates profit. The airline industry has found an equilibrium and the regulations require them to all do things much the same way.

The one thing airlines do not do well is to manufacture excess demand – if you want to fly, you can fly. Roughly speaking, all airlines are pretty similar and the number of people who want to fly on any given day is not dissimilar to the number of seats available on the planes. Imagine for a moment what would happen if half the planes in the world were suddenly grounded for a year. It's likely that those who could stay in the air would have a record profit. Nothing about their service would change, it's just the relationship between demand and supply that sets the price.

It's hard to accept but there's no such thing as objective value. Everything, absolutely all value, is subjective. We decide how much something is valued at based on how much we want it and how hard it is to get. If you wrote down all of the things you can do for your customers and then ask 1,000 people to put a value on it, you would probably get 1,000 different answers. Even if you ask just one person what they think your offer is worth, their answer might vary wildly, depending on what's happening in their life at the time and the way you present the offer.

If your offer seems like it's always available, to anyone who wants it and there's no indication of what it's value might be, you can guarantee people will devalue it.

Google Maps is an insanely valuable technology but it's given away for free. It's free because Google's ability to supply maps to people is infinite. The thing that is genuinely scarce is the ability to put a recommendation in front of a person at the precise moment they are looking for something. Because that is limited, Google can auction off those ads and the cost per click for certain terms can be astronomical.

Rolex watches are objectively overpriced for what they are. Why does a Rolex cost multiple times more than a Casio, Seiko or Longines? These alternatives are similar in materials, design, specifications and reliability. Why does Rolex make more profit than the rest of the mechanical watch industry combined? It's because they are not in the business of manufacturing watches, they are in the business of manufacturing demand for their watches.

When you walk into a Rolex retail store (known as dealerships or boutiques), the strangest thing happens, they won't let you buy the watch you want. Instead you must tell them what you want and then add your name to a waiting list. Months go by and you may get an occasional update that your 'name has moved up on the list' but your wrist is still void of the watch you desire. Eventually the day comes when you get a call from your 'Authorized Dealer' who informs you of the good news that your watch is available for purchase. There is, however, a caveat – you have just a few days to buy it or it will be sold to someone else. Rolex put just as much thought into the precision manufacturing of desire as they do to their timepieces.

In the Industrial Age, the ability to make things was very limited and the number of things people wanted was very high. People wanted more clothing, more books, more entertainment and more of everything else but for a long time very few businesses could manufacture those things fast enough. Not that long ago there were only a few dozen publishers of books, or only so many clothing stores dealing with a small cadre of sewing houses. Forget about making a film or a television show; that was so hard to do that even working in that industry was considered the stuff of dreams.

Not today. We have more than we can handle. We are making so many items of clothing that what we throw away is choking the rivers in Africa. We have such an abundance of books that there is now a word to describe a person who buys books they'll never read (tsundoku). As for entertainment, how many YouTube videos are piled up in your 'Watch Later' playlist? How many Netflix shows are you planning on getting to when you finally get snowed in? The options are endless and they continue to pile up. We all have way too much being supplied to us.

This means your business success is not dependent on your ability to supply something, it's your ability to manufacture demand for it that counts. The pendulum has swung from the supply side to the demand side receiving the rewards. As a business, you need to get good at building the assets of demand generation not just supply.

An assets of demand generation is anything that helps a customer to discover you, learn about your offer, gain trust in what you do, better understand how it will help them or feel better about buying from you. These assets are the things people typically experience very early in their journey with your business. It's not simply having traditional marketing materials, although they are essential. It's also appearing on podcasts, having a published book, releasing long videos on YouTube, building a following on Instagram. The true test is whether it's making people want what you offer. The assets that drive buying behaviour are far more important that the product people are buying.

Clients of mine, Joel and Sarah, have a clothing brand for teen girls called Dès Vu Clothing. Their primary product is an embossed hoodie that girls in the UK love wearing to the shops, to a party or around the house. It's a wildly profitable business not because hoodies are hard to make but because it's hard to make a teenage girl like a hoodie. Joel and Sarah are masters of social media. Their family has a YouTube channel featuring them and their five daughters having fun times. They have Instagram accounts and TikTok channels. They have established relationships with dozens of other influencers. All of these social media platforms feature Dès Vu hoodies and ramp up the desire people feel for the brand.

The hoodies aren't always available though. They release batches of these coveted fashion items in short bursts and when they sell out, they are gone. It's this winning formula of keeping demand outstripping supply that has made them a successful business. It's not hoodies that make money, it's the ability to manufacture demand for hoodies.

The key to manufacturing demand is campaigns. A great marketing campaign is a finite, high-energy burst of activity that focuses on one outcome. It is designed to collect buying signals, build tension until signalled demand exceeds supply, then create a moment to take action and buy. Getting into a rhythm of campaigns is the key to maintaining demand and supply tension all year around.

There are three campaigns I get businesses to run simultaneously. These three campaigns have also been the key to my growing businesses achieving their goals over the last 20 years. These are the three campaigns:

- **Perfect repeatable week:** This campaign repeats over and over, week after week. It's a mini-campaign designed to generate an ongoing build-up of sales opportunities. Over the last 20 years, I have run a weekly workshop, online assessments, book promotions and discussion groups as primary lead generators in my weekly campaigns. We put a lot of effort into creating ads, landing pages and offers that do not need changing regularly. Once we have our formula, we repeat it over and over and over again.

We measure four things on our perfect repeatable week 'LAPS dashboard' – leads, appointments, presentations and sales. We want the weeks to be smooth sailing so we know exactly what to expect and can plan accordingly.

Having helped hundreds of businesses set up a perfect repeatable week campaign, I can tell you the most successful ones centre on promoting a weekly workshop, online assessment, book giveaway, discussion group, mini-course, private dining experience, newsletter subscription or preregistration of interest. Each campaign is designed to get people to signal their interest in what you do. You can run ads, send e-mails or direct messages, sign up affiliate partners or create compelling content online to drive people to these campaigns. People fill in a form and let you know that they are interested and you can then turn that interest into a sale through further marketing or direct sales.

- **Quarterly spotlight:** Every 90 days your business wants to do something special that shines a spotlight on what your business can do. This campaign could take the form of a special live event, a limited-edition product or service, an experience, a collaboration or new product launch. When you plan these out across the year, they aren't stressful. These campaigns build up in the background of your perfect repeatable week. A prospect might talk to a salesperson and decide not to buy right away; this is an opportunity to invite them to the special spotlight event that's coming up next month. Conversely, someone might engage in your spotlight campaign, disappear for a few months and then re-engage with your weekly campaign.

For smaller businesses a spotlight campaign might be a private dining experience with a guest speaker. You could have a dozen people attend, raise some money for charity, showcase some success stories and partner with an interesting speaker. For a bigger business, you might run a full-day conference for 500 potential clients and partners. The Spotlight campaign can work at any scale to showcase the best parts of what you offer. It's also a great opportunity to capture photos or videos for your social media profiles.

- **Annual big message:** Throughout the year you want a few primary messages you want to become known for. These are big picture ideas – they're not focused on what you offer but why you do it. These campaigns happen across your social media platforms. Your business should have at least four active social media platforms and one of them is the primary place your customers will see you. You might have a YouTube channel, an Instagram and Facebook presence and then use LinkedIn as your dominant platform.

All of these platforms publish regular updates that serve the purpose of making it easy for people to find you and reminding people you exist. Most businesses massively underestimate how easily they're lost or forgotten amid the noise of modern life. Businesses that are really growing and succeeding post fresh content several times a week on their platforms. My business took off with our well-executed Perfect Repeatable Week but things grew tenfold when I committed to posting every single day on four platforms.

Your big message should be bold and inspiring. Focus on sharing the transformation your business delivers, focus on the memorable principles you stand for and the practical changes you help people to make. As you gain experience and confidence, you'll get better at creating content that hooks attention, holds it and even goes a little bit viral from time to time. This will be an important part of manufacturing demand for what you do.

Having assets that generate demand and running these three campaigns transformed my business. Early in my career, all I did was run repeatable weeks and I didn't develop or own many of the assets that were driving demand. I was going through the motions but year after year it got harder and harder to sustain. As soon as I started creating long-term assets that generated desire, life got easier and business became more fun. When I started campaigning with a big message and a quarterly spotlight a flywheel emerged. The spotlight campaigns helped us create more assets, which could be shared as part of the big message. The big message got more people engaging with our perfect repeatable weeks. The more people who engaged weekly, the easier it was to run something interesting as a spotlight campaign the following quarter. Around and around the flywheel goes making the business more and more in demand.

As entrepreneurs in a Digital Age, we don't make profit for creating wonderful products and services. We make a profit when we manufacture excess demand for our wonderful products and services.

Activity:

Go to ScoreApp.com and create a free account. Use the template library to set up an online assessment, waiting list or quiz to manufacture interest in your business or idea. Launch it and get 10 new leads for your business or idea.

AI prompt:

'I want to market what I do as if it is a rare, special luxury good. I want to heighten desire through powerful messaging and well-executed campaigns. Ask me questions to learn more about the key attributes of what I offer and then develop a campaign to get me oversubscribed. I want people to line up to buy from me. I want people to have a fear of missing out. I want them to have logical reasons for buying from me and emotional reasons for acting on their desires.'

CHAPTER 5

SHIFT 5: FROM PHYSICAL ASSETS TO DIGITAL ECOSYSTEMS

Mindset shift: Seeing digital assets like content and code as being valuable assets that you can develop and own.

As you fly into Dubai you can sense it is a city like no other. The giant palm-shaped island protruding into the gulf is a man-made feature that is visible from space. There are cranes everywhere, building the next luxury tower to adorn the desert. Standing tall in the middle of it all is the tallest building in the world, the Burj Khalifa. This almighty structure cost $1.5 billion and six years to construct. When all of its floors were sold, the total sale value was $2.7 billion, netting its developers $1.2 billion in gross profit. Spread across the six years of construction, this engineering marvel produced an average of $200 million of asset appreciation per year.

The creation of the Burj Khalifa sounds enormously impressive and lucrative but it pales in comparison to the value that can be created without a single day spent in the hot sun with a hard hat.

High above London on the 39th level of a Canary Wharf building two co-founders are pitching their new business, Revolut. It's 2015 and Nikolay Storonsky (ex-Credit Suisse trader) and Vlad Yatsenko (former Deutsche Bank engineer) are telling angel investors they intend to 'kill bank fees everywhere'. Although they intend to disrupt banks, they do not intend on opening any branches, fortifying any safes or leasing a fleet of security vans. Their initial idea is to use smartphones to allow travellers to hold multiple currencies at very low rates. They raised £1.5 million and began their journey building a business built purely on digital assets.

Six years into the Revolut journey the founders announced their business had raised £800 million of funding at a value of £33 billion. In the same time as it took to build the Burj Khalifa, these two founders had built something 12 times as valuable.

To this day, Revolut owns almost no physical assets. Even physical debit cards it issues are an optional extra, with most customers using their 'card' as an app on their phone.

Physical assets like buildings, land, stocks and machinery once comprised the bulk of a company's value – no longer is this the case. In the 1970s, accountants looked at the biggest 500 companies in the USA and found almost 20% of their value was not directly linked to physical items on their balance sheet. The accountants decided to call this added value discrepancy 'intangible value' or 'good will'. When we fast forward to 2025, the value of the S&P 500 is now comprised of 95% of this intangible value. If you were to liquidate most of the biggest companies in America you wouldn't have much physical stuff to sell – almost all of their value is stored in data centres, their brand, their contracts and their algorithms.

All over the world, the fastest growing and most valuable businesses are the ones that are focused on the creation of stuff that isn't actually stuff. Your lifestyle business must also focus on building assets in the digital world if you want to make the most of the times we are in. You could be successful with a local business that has a warehouse full of materials and a yard full of vehicles and equipment but it is a lot easier to create a highly profitable and scalable business that doesn't rely on these things. At the very least, if your business does rely on physical assets, make sure you surround it with as many digital assets as you can – give it a YouTube channel, a Customer Relationship Management (CRM) system, online payments and add some digital products. A business built on digital assets can interact and deliver value to more people and it's more valuable.

A digital asset is anything that would add value in your business if you and your team were to disappear. The most valuable digital assets are market-facing; they can be easily found online by anyone who's researching your business – especially the ones that manufacture demand – such as your website, social media accounts, videos, podcasts, books, awards, testimonials, scorecards or assessments, blogs, brand ambassadors and special landing pages.

Add to that things that aren't easy to see but add enormous value, such as your database, customer portal, AI agents, documented best practices, registered IP, e-mail campaigns, favourable contracts with suppliers, IT systems, independent reports and brand and culture book. If your business is brimming with these so-called intangible assets it's incredibly hard not to be growing and profitable.

Consider the difference in return you get from a digital asset versus a physical asset. If you were to buy a residential property or shares in large companies you could expect to see about 1–4% yield and 5–10% growth. If instead you invested in business assets you could see returns of over 100% and it could result in multiples of that in enterprise value.

I can share some personal examples. In 2017, I invested about $15,000 in creating the 24Assets.com website and assessment tool. In the following year it generated over $500,000 of new revenue as well as providing data with a long-term strategic value. Note: Today that asset could be set up far more easily and cheaply using ScoreApp.com.

In 2021, I engaged August Recognition to support us in entering and winning respected industry awards. It cost $10,000 for their team to conduct research and guide our submissions. In the following year we won three major awards and these awards helped us to win dozens of bigger contracts and attract A-players onto our team; I would estimate the value of these awards to be far more than $100,000.

In 2023, I invested $100,000 with Jammy Digital to ramp up my social media output. The results were staggering – our YouTube account gained tens of thousands of real subscribers, Instagram and LinkedIn exploded with over 100,000 followers each and we could measure financial results in the millions. With this level of online attention, we got flooded with organic leads equal to our $50,000 per month advertising budget and those leads were almost twice as likely to become clients.

Digital assets allow you to scale your value to far more people. Over 70% of the world's population has access to fast internet and digital assets allow you to be one click away from all of these people at the moment they care about what you do. Most entrepreneurs focus so heavily on what they do and neglect the importance of turning what they do into a digital asset.

I often ask entrepreneurs if they have every had a really happy customer. Almost all of them proudly nod their head while thinking about their favourite customer. Then I ask if they have captured this customer on video delivering an enthusiastic testimonial that is now on YouTube. Their face drops and they are embarrassed to say they haven't. I often ask people if they have delivered a talk to an audience and if they have captured it on video and posted it online. Those few that have, always report that their online audience is orders of magnitude greater than the number of people who saw the talk live.

They key to building digital assets is to create them with a long-term vision in mind. Short, sharp posts on X.com vanish within days but things like websites, landing pages, assessments, videos and testimonials can continue to do heavy lifting for your business years into the future. It's worth spending the money with high-quality suppliers to create long-term digital assets. I have found that the right suppliers bring in multiples of what they charge provided I brief them well and I don't expect them to have magic wands.

The real magic is not found in one new digital asset. It is the ecosystem of several assets working together that really produces profit and stability.

There are seven categories of digital assets a lifestyle business should develop:

- **Intellectual property assets:** This is based on your unique insights, stories, research and experiences. The best IP is impossible to copy or generate with AI because it flows from your life. This could take the form of content such as books, articles, videos, recordings or even frameworks and written methodologies. Your IP could also be legally protected IP like patents or registered trademarks.

To create more IP, pause, reflect and document. You are sitting on a goldmine of IP if you simply slow down and recognize it. Imagine a lawyer tells you that a relative has left you a house in their will but you have to travel a few hours to sign the paperwork – you'd be crazy not to block out some time to secure that asset in your name. Well it's equally as crazy not to formalize your experiences into IP. You've done all the hard work, the fun and easy bit is to document it. Go for a walk with a notepad and pen, find a bench and reflect on times that you have done something special, for a certain type of person, who got a remarkable result and you can explain it step by step. Then write it down, record a video or audio about it, design a framework for it and give it a unique name. You're on your way to having more IP – the building blocks of saleable value.

- **Brand assets:** Your brand is the way the world consistently experiences you and your business. At a basic level you and your business have a visual identity – you might have a style, fonts, colours and logos people associate to you. You also might have an underlying philosophy you're known for, perhaps a set of phrases or core values. Another powerful way to build a brand fast is through the personal brand of the founder and other brand ambassadors who embody similar values. Placing yourself and your business side by side with someone impressive has the effect of transferring their attributes onto you.

A trusted brand is a powerful asset, especially in an AI world where people are losing trust in everything they see, hear or read. It takes time to build a brand so the sooner you start the better. In order to show up consistently and powerfully, you must put some thought into formalizing your brand identity, philosophy and brand ambassador relationships. It's well worth creating a document called a brand guidelines booklet. This shows anyone involved in the business what you're aiming for; it gets your ideal brand choices out of your head and into a format people can replicate. Once people start to recognize and trust your brand, they naturally buy from you faster and in higher amounts. It's worth the investment to make your lifestyle business stand out for years to come.

- **Market assets:** These assets are about reaching more of the right people consistently. Channels to market, such as retailers, e-commerce stores or even YouTube channels, get you in front of more people more often. Positioning your business to be known for a particular thing people want means anyone searching for that outcome is likely to find you; you can do this through search engine optimization, winning awards and clear positioning statements in your marketing. Eventually you can also build your own database on a CRM and send e-mails or messages to them whenever you like.

As a rule, you can't have too many ways to reach your market. Don't wrestle deciding between e-commerce or retail partnerships, do both. Don't be afraid to set up too many landing pages or lead magnets, so long as they all add people to a central CRM, the more the better. Have a mini-course, an assessment, a discussion group and a love webinar registration page; let them each bring in hundreds of warm leads per month. Enter awards. Once you are an award-winning business, you'll have more customers finding you and it's easier to make sales. Some people say awards are silly, but not the people who win them. All of these assets result in more people beating a path to your door.

- **Product assets:** At the core of your business are the products and services you sell. Each one needs its own digital assets such as a brochure, landing page and explainer video. Very few products or services are clear to customers on their own merits and in a digital world, if a customer can't easily get a clear understanding of what they are buying on their screens, they aren't buying it.

Many businesses expect customers to be mind readers and somehow know exactly what they will get. Put yourself in the customer's shoes, imagine them being bombarded with special offers from a range of companies while they are trying to make a selection on what to buy or who to sign up with as a client. They might also need to get buy-in from a colleague or spouse. Have you made it effortless for them to find everything they need on their phone? You want it to be easy for them to pass their phone to their friend and show them what to buy. The upside in creating these product assets is that you and your team will also gain enormous clarity about the value you offer in the process of compiling these assets.

Treat everything you sell as if it were a product that could be sold or delivered on the other side of the world. The hit musical *Book of Mormon* runs in the USA, UK, Australia and Italy. The cast and crew change but the customer experience is identical. They have productized it. Every service can be designed in a standardized, packaged format with fixed prices and deliverables. At this point, the digital collateral used to promote it can also be standardized and scaled without significant changes.

- **Systems assets:** A business needs to run as efficiently as possible. You need a 'best-way of doing it' for everything in your business. Without this, you and your team waste too much time making things up or messing things up. Some businesses are so good at systems, it's their primary asset. Many restaurants and cafes can make a better burger than McDonald's but no one has mastered the systems of running a burger restaurant better. Your business will be worth more if you run on tight systems. It has never been easier to achieve this – there are software platforms dedicated to automating and systematizing almost every aspect of every business, leaving you to focus on the special and unique elements of what you do. Anything you don't know, you can ask an AI – 'what are the established best-practices for doing [activity] within my [type/industry] business?' – and you will get the base-level systems thinking that already exists.

There are three types of systems you need to have a successful operation. Most importantly, you need sales and marketing systems – in order to drive leads, sales and referrals to your business. Secondly, you'll need your customer fulfilment systems to remarkably look after your clients, provide great customer service and deliver your product or service to such a high standard that people tell their friends. Thirdly, you need management systems to run your organization – progress can be tracked, accounts are accurate, departments have viability of their key numbers and individual team members can be guided towards more valuable outcomes. These valuable systems are mostly based on software you can subscribe to cheaply and then plug in your unique approach. Systems are intangible but they're worth more than gold.

- **Culture assets:** Businesses with great culture assets attract the right people to build and grow the business with. These assets are key for recruiting and retaining team members who are eager to contribute their skills to add value to the company, and who want to continue training and developing their skills to improve their performance. Having this kind of team encourages others to want to join, stay and develop a sense of loyalty to the company. With great culture assets, your business will have members who stay on longer than other people in the same role would for the average company. You'll also get people who are better qualified for the role looking to join your team. Your business will attract, train and develop great talent constantly, making it easy for you to build and retain the best people in their fields.

Culture is routed in behaviour not words. Your business might say 'we are dynamic' on the website but if it takes you a month to make a decision that could have been made in a few days, your culture says otherwise. A strong sales culture can be observed when you see a sales team hitting the phones and following the sales scripts, a culture of excellence is observed when you see a team celebrating a 1% gain, a culture of customer care is visible when a customer writes a review about how their complaint was resolved fast and the person they spoke to went above and beyond for them. Your culture assets need to embed and celebrate these behaviours.

- **Funding assets:** Every business hits a point where it would benefit from access to funding. At a small scale this could take the form of an overdraft or credit terms with suppliers. At a bigger level you might want to attract angel investors or private equity partners who can invest the money you need to unlock serious growth. Funding requires documentation from credible sources. Creating financial forecasts, business plans, management accounts, risk-mitigation reports and independent valuations can move you a lot closer to unlocking funds.

  Producing funding assets requires you to seek assistance from professionals. There's a language of money communicated through spreadsheets and reports that are signed off by people with independence and credibility.

The process of creating these assets is hugely valuable. Creating a painfully detailed financial forecast of your business with an experienced business analyst can transform your whole strategy. Fortunately you can find these professionals online and engage them directly at affordable rates for a small lifestyle business. The true test of your funding assets is the access you gain to deeper pockets to grow your business.

You probably grew up in a time where physical assets were the most important and productive building blocks of the economy. Now it's about digital assets that cannot be found in the real world other than on the pixels they light up on a screen and the neurons they fire off in people's brains. It's strange but the people who are worth the most money and have the most freedom are the people whose assets are intangible – barely more than an idea that has been documented, formalized and stored on a hard-drive in a random data-centre somewhere. Ones and zeros are worth a lot more than concrete and steel today.

Activity:
Visit www.24assets.com and take the assessment to discover the ecosystem of assets your current business has. Read through the free report and action the recommendations. If you do not have an existing business, offer to do this activity with an entrepreneur you know.

AI prompt:

'I want to develop high-quality digital assets that are unique to me. Ask me questions to identify potential assets I could create. Develop a step-by-step plan for me to create a coherent ecosystem.'

CHAPTER 6

SHIFT 6:
FROM BUSINESS BRANDS
TO PERSONAL BRANDS

> **Mindset shift: From believing big brands have all the power to recognizing the significant power in your personal brand.**

Cristiano Ronaldo casually walks into the briefing room in Budapest to face dozens of eager journalists. He's there for the pre-match press conference of the Euro 2020 final. The press conference has not officially started but the cameras are rolling.

As he sits down and gets comfortable he notices two perfectly placed Coca-Cola bottles placed in front of him. Ronaldo, a father and a symbol of health and fitness, gives the bottles a disapproving glance and proceeded to slide them out of view. Off camera, he notices someone who is clearly worried about this, Coca-Cola has spent €30 million to be the official sponsor of the tournament. In response to their anguish, he proudly holds up a clear bottle and says 'aqua' and places it down in the shot.

Ronaldo is one of the most influential personalities in the world. At this time he has over 500 million followers on his personal Instagram account. Contrast this to Coca-Cola – despite the 135-year-old mega-corporation being one of the biggest advertisers in the world – just 2.7 million people are following their account. Across all platforms Ronaldo's brand gets five times the viewership of Coca-Cola and he doesn't have to spend a cent.

The whole incident lasted less than 30 seconds but it sent a clear message. The video was shared on social media and started a global conversation among football fans and health enthusiasts. The tag #aqua began trending on social media alongside #euro2020. The following day Coca-Cola's share price dropped 1.6%, wiping $4 billion of value off their market capitalization.

Personal brands are far more powerful than business brands in the digital age. Our brains evolved to form emotional attachments to people not words and symbols. This is why Kylie Jenner effortlessly dethroned Revlon with her makeup brand. Ryan Reynolds was able to explode the value of Mint Mobile by 50,000% in two years. Jimmy Donaldson (aka MrBeast) is the greatest threat to Cadbury's. Rihanna was able to build her lingerie brand, Fenty, into something worth double their rival Victoria's Secret in just a few years.

In the Industrial Age, people didn't have a platform without approval from large corporations. It was impossible for someone to communicate directly with the fans and followers unless someone at a large established brand gave them the platform to do so. Even then it was carefully produced, edited or even deleted to fit the agenda of the organization. The Beatles were the most famous faces in the 1960s but even they had no way of talking directly to a mass market unless the media gave them the green light.

Social media profoundly changed this. Every person, including you, has the power to talk directly to everyone else in the world. It can't be overstated what an awesome opportunity this has created. Your lifestyle business will be linked to your personal brand. Like it or not, as an entrepreneur you will be the face of your business and if you resist it, you will be competing with someone whose personal brand is growing at speed.

In the Industrial Age, the way to position a business was at the intersection of a geographical location and the products or services. A hair salon in Houston. A plumber in Pennsylvania. A law firm in Los Angeles. All you needed to know about a business was its name, location and what it did. Geography offered a natural niche positioning and since most businesses had a physical location, a business brand was sufficient. Before Google, the *Yellow Pages* listed the business brands under each product or service category and that is how people found what they were looking for.

In the Digital Age, most fast-growth businesses and lifestyle businesses are not fixed to a location. They can deliver products and services to people in many places. As a result they want their message to spread to anyone who could benefit from it. The best way to do this is through social media and these platforms are not friendly to business brands or to people who only talk about what they sell. For this reason you must position your business at the intersection of your unique intellectual property and the ideal customer you serve. At this intersection, rather than putting a faceless business brand, you put yourself as the representative of the business. The way people discover you today is through your story, your ideas and through clearly identifying the ideal customer you serve. All of this is delivered by you as the key person of influence.

You may feel a sense of resistance about this. You might not want to be stopped on the street for autographs, you might feel self-conscious about the way you look on screen – maybe you associate having a personal brand to being a shameless self-promoter.

None of that needs to hold you back. You're not going to be sharing pictures of your breakfast, revealing details of your personal life or leasing a Ferrari in a ploy to get more followers. What you will need to do is to shine a spotlight on your business and what it can do. You won't be saying 'look at me' you will be saying 'look at that'. It must, however, be you that is saying it. The voice of you, the founder, will be orders of magnitude more powerful than the faceless brand of your business.

If you want to enjoy the fruits of a lifestyle business, it's time to throw away your reservations and position yourself as a key person of influence in your industry. A key person of influence is not a celebrity and they're not an influencer seeking followers as a key measure of success. They are a business leader who represents their business and brand powerfully. They take to the stage, screen and page to give their business a voice and get cut-through in a noisy market.

You're seeing these key people of influence every time you go online. They are unique individuals but they have a lot in common.

They are great talkers. They talk directly to camera. They hook your attention, they discuss real problems and offer up solutions and if you want to dive deep they make it easy for you. They are clear about what they focus on and they make a compelling case for it.

They have a book. Maybe they have several books out. You might not have read their book but you know they wrote it. It signals that they must seriously care about their topic. If you don't have time to read their book, you can dive deep into their long form social posts, videos, podcasts and special reports.

They are selling something. It's not a hard sell but their products are just a few clicks away. They might offer software, training, a full-service agency or physical products they can ship to your door.

They've got followers and subscribers. Click over to their profile and you'll see you're not the only one who's taking an interest. Some have thousands of followers, some have hundreds of thousands or even millions of people who are taking an active interest. They also speak at industry conferences, they are guests on podcasts and get featured in relevant newsletters or blogs.

They're not acting alone. They have a team around them and they are good friends with the who's who of their industry. In fact they aren't just friends, they all seem to collaborate and promote each other. The very people you might think would be their competitors are smiling in photos with them.

These key people of influence are taking over every industry with their small but powerful personal brands. You already know of these people in your industry – their names keep coming up in conversations and you can't avoid them in your social media feed. They seem to be attracting opportunities, having a lot of fun and making vastly more money than most.

All of these people are normal humans. They all started out feeling a bit awkward in front of a camera, they all felt reticent to share opinions at first and they all started out with zero people following them. You could become a key person of influence in your industry too – it's something you must focus on if you want to have a business that delivers you a great lifestyle.

Since 2010, my focus has been on developing the personal brands of entrepreneurs. I wrote one of the first books on the topic, *Key Person of Influence*, and have had a hands-on impact with over 5,000 founders and leaders to achieve a breakthrough using their personal brand as a growth lever.

The proven framework is to focus on five keys to becoming a key person of influence: pitching, publishing, products, profile and partnerships.

- **Pitching** – your ability to speak powerfully about your business, to enrol others into your ideas and get them to take new actions as a result of your words. You can pitch your ideas in writing, in a conversation, on a stage or a screen. The important part is that your words have influence. You aren't just explaining what you do, you are capturing attention and moving people in the direction of your business. With a great pitch, your words have the power to build an audience, attract customers, secure investment, cement a partnership or even start a movement.

Entrepreneurship is the journey of 1,000 pitches. If you are building a business, you are going to pitch it over and over and over again. Unfortunately the penalty for being average at pitching has never been so severe. If you deliver 1,000 average pitches you will have almost nothing to show for it. The payoff for powerful pitching has never been so immense. Powerful pitches gather pace like an avalanche down a mountain. One great pitch to an individual can create a customer and also a referral; then you get invited to pitch to an audience at an event, then you find yourself pitching on a video that is seen by thousands of people and then you are featured on a podcast watched by millions.

Crafting your pitch as an entrepreneur is akin to a professional tennis player practising their serve until it is unstoppable. Like a comedian refines their jokes and the delivery to get maximum laughs, an entrepreneur must refine the pitch for maximum impact. An entrepreneur who hasn't dedicated serious time and attention to their pitch is doomed to fail in the wake of those who do. Your first step in building your personal brand is to upgrade the way you pitch.

- **Publishing** – your ability to create content that engages people and draws them to your business. Once you have developed your pitch, you must publish your ideas so you can build relationships at scale. By definition, publishing is the way you put your ideas into the public domain. You can do this with written words, videos or audio that is made freely available online. It should be effortless to discover what you stand for if someone goes looking online.

Humans have the ability to form 'para-social relationships'. These are the relationships we imagine we have with celebrities, public figures, authors or people we follow online. The one-sided relationships are formed when we consume published content from people we don't personally know in the real world. You have done this yourself throughout your life – as you read a book, watched a podcast and followed a social media account your brain was making a connection with someone who doesn't know you exist.

Research from Professor Robin Dunbar on how we bond indicates that interacting with people online for seven hours is enough to form a bond that is strong enough for you to remember the person and what they are about for months, maybe years into the future. If you can build this strong relationship with thousands of people, your business will thrive.

One of the most powerful tools for building relationships at scale is to write a book. When you are an author, you become an authority. Even if few people read your book, people know you have written it and that counts for a lot. I researched the guest list of the popular podcast 'Diary of a CEO' and discovered 78% of the guests had written a book. Given less than 1.5% of the general population are authors, it speaks to the power of being an author to gain access to bigger platforms. To have a lifestyle business your ability to publish your ideas into books, blogs, podcasts, videos and other online assets is a cornerstone skill.

- **Products** – your ability to monetize your idea and influence through well-crafted offers. Your personal brand gains or loses strength as a result of the products and services you associate with. Many online influencers do not have products and services of their own and they are at the whims of sponsors and partners who offer financial incentives to promote (often subpar) deals. Key people of influence have their own select ecosystem of products and services they have created and are proud to represent. The key person of influence isn't getting paid to promote something, they are an owner of the business that offers something they truly believe in.

What you offer must be scalable to a global audience. It's pointless building a global following who are unable to buy from you. The products and services your offer should either be delivered online or be able to ship to main markets. Software solutions, training, consulting, diagnostics, books and services that can be delivered remotely are ideal. Alternatively, physical products that do not get easily damaged, perish, aren't heavily regulated or commoditized are great places to start – there's a reason clothing, merchandise, supplements and small homewares are leading e-commerce categories.

Products and services don't make profit, product and service ecosystems do. It's ideal to build a family of products and services associated to your personal brand. It's easy for a competitor to replicate a single product but hard to compete with an elegant suite of products and services. Key people of influence who have a book, keynote speech, consulting, software and a membership are hard to compete with. On their own, each of those products don't make a fortune but put them all together and they become a commercial force.

- **Profile** – your ability to be seen by a large number of people in your addressable market. You are who Google or ChatGPT says you are when a prospect searches for your name. If nothing accurate comes up, it's your fault not the search results. You might be technically brilliant at what you do but if that isn't easily discovered you are selling yourself at a massive discount.

  When someone searches you out, they want to see a range of indicators that tell them if you have a recognized profile. They will look at what you have posted on social media and how many people follow you. They'll see if you've won awards or worked with brands they admire. They will see if you have spoken at industry events and if there are videos of you sharing your ideas. They'll look at the view count and in the comments to see how people react to you. They'll see if you have been featured in the media or on well-known blogs, podcasts or YouTube channels. To the degree that you are visible and seen by your peers as valuable, you will be able to charge more and do business with more people.

For most lifestyle businesses, a following of 5,000–50,000 people on social media will be plenty to keep your sales pipeline full of opportunities. This respectable number of people puts you above most in your industry; it gives you a platform of people you can reach with a message and it's achievable for anyone who has something interesting to say. The key is consistently showing up and saying it on your platforms and those you get invited onto.

- **Partnerships** – your ability to forge mutually beneficial arrangements with others in your industry. Someone woke up this morning with the resources you wish you had. Far better than competing with them or trying to replicate what they have, is to create a partnership to access their value. If someone has fame, you can do a brand ambassador partnership with them to use your products and services as a way for them to monetize their influence. If someone has a PhD qualification, you could add them to your advisory board so they have another outlet for their knowledge and they can monetize their credibility. If someone has a lot of money, you can partner with them as an angel investor so they can get a return on their capital or use their capital to develop a business they care about. Creating partnerships is a powerful way to build and utilize your personal brand.

A friend and client, Pedro Pimenta became a quadruple amputee at 19 years old. One day he was feeling a bit unwell, the next thing he remembers is waking up in a hospital bed being told that he almost died from meningitis. It had cost him both arms and both legs. For many months after the operation, Pedro believed he would spend the rest of his life dependent on his family for even the most basics of life.

One day he decided to transform the way he saw his situation and he committed himself to learning the skills required to run his own life. Pedro didn't just teach himself how to walk, shave, drive and even snowboard again. He also decided to launch a rehabilitation clinic for amputees.

Pedro recognized that his story had enormous power and he wrote a book, started giving talks and built a social media account to show how he conquers everyday challenges. His DaVinci Clinic in Brazil has become a destination for amputees from around the world to learn the advanced skills they need to live life on their terms. Pedro has forged partnerships with hospitals, charities and funders from all over the world and has secured investment to open several locations.

Less than 1 in 150 people suffer any form of traumatic amputation and by its nature, it's not easy to find or reach many of these people. Until recently, a destination clinic specializing in this issue would have been a near-impossible venture to make viable. Through the power of social media, Pedro can connect with the global community of people who have lost a limb.

Instead of being defeated by his condition, he has recognized his power to be a key person of influence to people around the world. At any other time in history, Pedro wouldn't have had the ability to build a personal brand and lifestyle business. Today, his personal brand is developing and his business is booming because all of the technology is available to connect with anyone from anywhere in the world. He even shares with me that he wouldn't change a thing about what happened because of the impact he's having in the world. He jokes that he would have probably ended up working as a boring accountant and it was worth at least an arm and a leg to avoid that life.

Your personal brand doesn't require you to experience something as dramatic as what happened to Pedro. You only need to recognize that your story is unique, you've had experiences that others can relate to, you know how to solve problems that others experience and you have the technology freely available to connect with your people wherever they are in the world.

Your business brand will become relevant as an extension of your personal brand. It will become the brand for the community of people who have bought from you because they relate to your story. Eventually your business brand may take on a life of its own, as it did for Enzo Ferrari, Walt Disney or Coco Chanel. For now, grow your business brand through your personal brand and enjoy the opportunities it opens up.

Activity:

Visit https://scorecard.dent.global to take the online self-assessment to measure and improve your ability to build a personal brand. Get the free report and action the specific recommendations for you.

AI prompt:

'Help me to become a key person of influence in the industry I am passionate about. Ask me questions and then develop a step-by-step strategy that will raise my profile within a niche community of the right people who will resonate with my story. Suggest further resources and tools I can leverage.'

CHAPTER 7

SHIFT 7: FROM ENDLESS GROWTH TO HAVING ENOUGH

Mindset shift: No longer will you endlessly chase growth for its own sake. Instead you will design the life you want and appreciate that success happens at the point where more money or a bigger business wouldn't meaningfully add to your lifestyle.

'What does it feel like to be born into a super-rich family?', I ask.

I watch as the face of the 25-year-old sitting opposite me contorts for a second. He awkwardly smiles, then he looks sad and then he quickly composes himself.

'No one really asks me that directly', he starts.

'It's strange. It's like being handed a priceless piece of art and my whole life is already planned out so that I'm not the one who destroys it. My main job is just to make sure it's protected and then hand it on to my kids', he says.

This young man is a fascinating guy I've come to know and catch up with from time to time. His grandfather founded a business that is now a household name brand that employs over 20,000 people. To this day his family owns a couple hundred million dollars' worth of the stock along with several houses, boats, a plane and massive commercial real estate portfolio across the USA. Every month, millions of dollars hit the bank account comprising of rent and dividends. This money then goes out to maintain a high standard of living for the entire family – money is allocated to the family's philanthropic activities and the rest is automatically reinvested. They have developed a system of compounding wealth and protecting themselves from all sorts of losses.

Apparently no one has asked my friend directly what it's like being a beneficiary of this system for a while because he wants to open up. 'Nothing I do really matters. I've had ideas to start a business but it's stupid to even begin it because I don't think it would make a difference and I'd only be taking away an opportunity for someone else. I've tried giving money away but it's harder than it looks to do properly and my family are already pretty good at it. I've tried making investments but they all have to be run past our investment committee and they always have better ideas. I don't actually know what I even want to do with my life. I suppose I can do anything but it all feels really meaningless given my circumstances', he laments.

Not having enough is a problem many people can relate to; having too much is also a problem but few people understand it.

When you have too much, the fun goes away. You are forced to become an asset manager. You are forced to screen people out of your life. You have to keep your guard up. People who have too much often struggle with addictions, vices, boredom, low self-esteem and trusting others. Ironically, they suffer with many of the afflictions we see in those who have too little.

There is wisdom in knowing when to stop. When enough is enough.

This is a lesson I am sharing with you not because I have found the balance myself but because I failed to. I grew up in a home where lack of money was a regular conversation I was privy to. I moved out of my family home at 18 and found myself barely surviving week to week on my wits. I launched my first company on my credit cards and scaled into the millions of revenue without taking on any funding by pouring everything back into my business. I boomed and busted three (almost four) times. As a result of this, I sit on a nagging feeling that I don't have enough and I need to keep chasing more in order to be secure.

I compulsively start new businesses, grow into new territories, launch new products and hire more people. I delay my own happiness or enjoyment in the moment so that I can try to make my family's future more secure. Even as a millionaire in my forties, I often think about how I will survive later in life. I imagine negative scenarios I might need to prepare for. I feel responsible for everything I can imagine my kids will face in their lifetimes. I feel guilty when I see problems in the world and I'm not personally doing something about it. I compare myself to my heroes who have achieved far more than me. I struggle to say no to people or opportunities.

This isn't a healthy way to live. This tendency not to recognize the point of enough resulted in having health issues relating to chronic stress. I often need reminding that things are OK, I'm doing fine and it's safe to enjoy the moment without running straight to the next thing. If it wasn't for my wife, I would have almost no healthy relationship with the concept of enough. It's her positive influence that has resulted in me finally getting my bearings.

Having ventured past the point where complexity and stress are adequately compensated, I want you to avoid the same mistakes. I want you to be better than I was at recognizing when you have enough.

The goal in life is not the accumulation of resources. It's not about taking on every problem or seizing every opportunity. It's about fun, freedom, flexibility, family, friendships, fitness and flow. What would be the point of being a billionaire if your experience of life was lonely, guarded, stressed out and detached? If you hated the problems you had to solve, if you didn't trust the people in your life, if your health was suffering and you felt trapped in it all, would the money really be a reward? Of course not.

Fun, freedom and fulfilment are the new success metrics for entrepreneurial teams

So how much is enough?

For one couple I know, they each have 12 coaching clients per year who pay $8,000 per client. They work for three weeks of the month and travel somewhere nice for a week without checking their phones or emails. This couple have their normal home in the city and a cottage in the countryside. They have nice but normal cars and they fly economy. They could work harder, they could launch new products and services and save up to buy bigger homes, fancier cars and fly business class but they've decided that they have enough. They have found the point where it's all fun and in alignment with their broader goals of health, family and regular travel.

Another couple I know have a massive villa with a Rolls Royce, a Ferrari and a 4×4 Lamborghini parked out the front. They have a 100-ft yacht, an art collection, they fly private or first class. They have countless watches and jewellery in their safe. They used to own a private jet but it was too stressful to own and maintain so they got rid of it. What's interesting is that they also have enough. They balance all of this wealth with their health and fitness, their family life and their friendships. Their wealth isn't a burden and it doesn't weigh them down. It just happens to be the case that the things they are good at pay extremely well.

A gentleman I know is insanely rich. He keeps starting companies, scaling them up and selling them for mind blowing amounts of money. Unfortunately it's stopped making him feel a sense of satisfaction. When we catch up he tells me that what he really wants is to meet the right woman and start a family. He tells me he will do this after the next company sells. He's been telling me this for many years and several companies have already sold.

A friend got paid for a consulting job in Bitcoin back in 2013. His wealth soared and he decided that what he really wanted was to buy a block of land, build a home with his own hands and raise a family in a forest. His house is modest, he could afford to buy more land and a bigger house if he wanted to. He could travel or invest in startups but he's found the point of contentment.

Having enough is not a set number. It's about finding the point where the juice is no longer worth the squeeze. It's a process of discovery based on your skills, passions and vision. It's something you can feel as well as calculate.

No matter who you are or what you have, you will know someone who has more. Someone will have more wealth, more liquidity, more toys, more holidays and more impact than you. Even in the ranks of billionaires, the people who have a billion dollars know people who have ten billion. The people with ten billion know people with twenty billion. Even Elon Musk, when asked about his massive fortune, said that he wasn't as liquid as other billionaires and that he couldn't do things that world leaders of nations could do. Someone will always have more and if you don't put a boundary in place, enough will never be enough.

No matter what you achieve, another milestone will always be within reach. I remember what it felt like to hit a million revenue per year. I had previously imagined that I would be satisfied with that forever – I wasn't. Today, I have businesses producing more than a million per month and I see a path to $100 million per year. I remember what it was like to hit 10,000 followers on social media, then 50,000 and then 100,000. Each time I thought it would be enough but each time I realized how with just a little more effort I could get to the next milestone. The next achievement will always seem within reach and it will always seem worth it. In reality, you can become trapped on a treadmill of endless achievement with diminishing levels of satisfaction. You're not imagining it – that's how things work and you have to set boundaries if you want to finally have enough.

Money can only solve problems that money solves. There are many problems that money can help with but can't solve for you. Your health is a major one – you can get help with your health but ultimately you have to focus on it or you'll lose it. The same can be said for important relationships – your executive assistant can't build a relationship with your kids for you. You can't outsource adventures – if you don't take time out to experience new things in new places you miss out. A sense of gratitude isn't bought – it comes when you slow down and reflect on how fortunate you already are. Inspiration isn't on offer from Amazon.com – you get inspired when you clarify your vision away from the endless cycles and loops you are caught in. A quiet mind, a loving relationship and a healthy body require your attention. All of these things only happen when you have temperance.

In a digital world of abundance, you have to learn the skill of having enough. Without contemplating where this point is, you will face an endless barrage of suggestions of places you must go, things you must buy, goals you must attain and people you must meet. When industrialized food manufacturing took off, the world saw an obesity epidemic. People couldn't control their primal desires to consume more calories. The same thing is happening with the online world – force-feeding us an unnatural sense of what a good life must include.

The key to having a lifestyle business is to recognize when to diversify your interest. Yes you are an entrepreneur and that's an important part of your life but you are also many other things. You are part of a family, you have a body that needs taking care of, you are a big kid who wants to play and have fun, you are a lover of music and of books. You adore great food, walks in nature and time spent on the floor building Lego.

Through the business accelerator we run at Dent Global, I have had the unique opportunity to get close with hundreds, maybe thousands of entrepreneurs, and see what their lives are really like when they let their guard down. I've been very close with people who are starting something new, running an established firm, scaling up a tech company or selling a business for hundreds of millions.

The most common example I see of someone who is very happy is someone who has a business with a team of 4–12 people, including them. The team is fluid and flat in its structure. Problems get solved quickly and there are very few pointless meetings or erroneous reports to do. These businesses leverage intellectual property, media, data and technology really well. They seem a lot bigger than they are from the outside and on the inside they feel light and lean.

These boutique businesses are so wonderful to own because they offer the best of all words. They are not lonely nor are they crowded. Each person gets to focus on their strengths but not to the point of being a cog in a machine. There are plenty of ideas and it doesn't seem impossible to get things done. If someone takes a holiday or gets sick, there are people who can cover for them. These businesses don't typically have demanding shareholders or lenders to answer to. The 4–12 person boutique is the most common size of a lifestyle business.

The self-employed or solopreneur life is rarely the dream lifestyle. Everything is on your shoulders. Marketing campaigns, you. Sales calls, you. Content marketing, bookkeeping, IT issues, setting up with suppliers, making customers happy, scheduling meetings, checking contracts, all on you. If you want to take a holiday, the whole business is now on holiday – can you imagine what would happen if Tim Cook sent every Apple employee on holiday all at once.

Solo-entrepreneurs and even founders with teams of up to three people, never fully get to take a break. Each person represents such a big part of the business – it's not realistic that the business can function without a person for long without something breaking. A team of one to four people is typically stretched. Everyone is juggling too many balls and it's common for them to drop.

A small team of 4–12 people, armed with AI capability, solves this and makes it all the more fun. With a team of 4–12, the business has enough people that an absence can be covered for. The founder can take a holiday and actually switch off in the knowledge that the team has their back. With 4–12 people, each person can focus and start to specialize in the thing they are good at. The marketing person can generate warm leads in the knowledge that the salesperson will close sales. No one has to wear so many hats that they start to spiral downwards.

The dynamic changes after 12 people. Rather than one team, you have teams of teams. Then you need a leadership team, then you need investment, then you need more people to live up to the expectations you set for investors, then you need a human resources manager and then it keeps growing in size and complexity or it hits a wall. Either way, it's not the easy, fun thing it used to be.

Unless you are totally sure that you want to build a much bigger business of at least 30+ people, I would advise almost every entrepreneur to shoot for a 4–12 person boutique. If you go bigger be prepared for it to capture a lot more of your time and energy. Be ready for meetings about the meetings. Be ready to check over people's reports and updates and give feedback. Be ready for a dozen people to want a quick chat with you each week. Yes, a bigger business can make more money and it can even sell for a life-changing amount of money if all goes to plan, but it comes with costs.

You're looking for a life that's fun. Fun is an indicator that your nervous system is enjoying the ride. Somehow in our human evolution, our bodies created the feeling of having fun. It stirs up when you feel safe, surrounded by trusted people, doing something engaging with the right amount of challenge. You react with easy ability to laugh, focus and create. Pay attention if the journey doesn't feel very fun.

In this digital, AI-powered economy, your lifestyle business can and should present to you three key gifts:

- **Creative freedom** – you can work on projects that inspire you with the types of people you have good chemistry with. You can say no to people or projects that bring your energy down. You feel that you are growing as a person through your work and that your output is meaningful to the world.
- **Financial freedom** – you can live comfortably with enough that your decisions aren't primarily motivated by paying your bills. You can forecast into the future and see that your ability to live and provide is getting better and better. You do not feel indebted to anyone. You can take

time off for holidays and hobbies without feeling it desta-
bilizes your finances.

- **Geographical freedom** – you are not trapped in one
place, it would not greatly affect your business to change
country if you chose to. You are not controlled by any
government unless you choose to be and you can easily
change your place of residence if it becomes too oppres-
sive where you live.

Many entrepreneurs do not feel they can enjoy these
three gifts because their business doesn't allow for it. The
reality is it's your business and you make the rules. You are
the one who designs your business. If you aren't happy with
what it's providing, acknowledge that it is a sub-optimal
design and you are free to recreate it. You are living in a time
of awesome abundance. Starting from scratch, many people
can build a lifestyle business in a year or two. Do not accept
being bored, broke or bound to one place.

The Industrial Age was built on the principle of endless
growth. Most businesses required a lot of capital to start
and the capital came with conditions of repaying it with
interest or providing a big return for investors. As the businesses grew, they needed even more financing and refinanc-
ing to produce stock, open up new locations, hire armies of
workers or develop new technology. It was an endless treadmill that required non-stop growth just to stay afloat.

The Digital Age is different. You don't need massive startup costs. The technology is available for free or
for a small subscription cost. You don't need to open new

locations to reach customers all over the world. Even when you are a global business you won't require many people on your team. For this reason, your business won't be on a treadmill of endless growth – you are free to choose when enough is enough. Once your business reaches the point where you are loving the lifestyle your business provides, you can decide to have the one thing most billionaires never reach – enough.

Activity:

Explore your rules for having enough in a journal or note in your phone. At what point will you decide that you have achieved a lifestyle business? When you reach that point, how will you diversify your interests? What are some of your beliefs or goals that have the potential to drive you beyond the point of good judgement? Who do you respect and admire because they have achieved enough and they relish their moments? What level of insurance, savings or investments would put your mind at ease around safety and security?

AI prompt:

'Act as a wealth planner. Ask me questions to discover the exact amount of money I need to live the life I aspire to while also paying taxes and provisioning for retirement. Ask me questions to discover my best options for reaching my goals through a boutique lifestyle business that generates cash flow in a predictable way.'

PART II

THE PLAYBOOKS

The locals thought they were crazy. Two grown men, both in their thirties, standing on the beach with their arms outstretched, their eyes squinting and their hair whipping around their face in the wind. They had been there for hours, feeling the way the wind pushed their arms up and down with every slight adjustment to the angles of their hands. Kitty Hawk had one of the windiest places in America and the brothers had travelled 700 miles from their home in Ohio to be there, which in 1900 was no joke. Travelling long distances wasn't easy before the invention of airplanes – Orville and Wilbur Wright were on the cusp of changing that forever. They may have looked foolish in that moment but they were discovering the principles of aerodynamics that would give humanity the power to fly.

The first aircraft were dangerous and unreliable. The Wright brothers achieved just 12 seconds of flight on the morning of 17 December 1903. By the afternoon they had achieved 59 seconds of controlled, powered flight before a gust of wind damaged their aircraft beyond repair.

In the years immediately following the Wright brothers' first takeoff, the pursuit of powered flight was both exhilarating and deadly. From 1903 to the outbreak of World War I in 1914, it's estimated that over 100 pilots, engineers and passengers died in flight-related accidents. Considering how few people were involved in this pioneering endeavour, strapping into the cockpit of a plane was almost suicide.

Today the opposite is true. People who are enjoying in-flight entertainment at this moment are some of the safest people in history. You are safer in a plane than walking down the street – by a lot. If you wanted to die in a plane crash, you would have to fly every day for 26,000 years for it to be statistically likely. How did we go from something being impossible, to being insanely dangerous, to being commonplace and predictably safer than walking in under a century?

We discovered the playbooks for flight. We understand aerodynamics, we have preflight checklists, we stick to maintenance schedules and when the slightest things go wrong new systems are developed. There are countless ways to build a plane that won't fly and only a few dozen designs that work. There are thousands of dumb mistakes you can make during takeoff or landing that will get people killed. The key to success is to stick to what does work. Don't go back to trial and error, don't stand on the beach flapping your arms, don't repeat the failures of the past. Build on top of a set of principles that work.

Entrepreneurship is similar to flight. It was very risky to be an entrepreneur and many people have wiped themselves out financially in pursuit of a business success story. Along the way, we've found a set of playbooks that make entrepreneurship safe – done well, it's safer than having a job at a big established corporation, earns more money and is a lot more fun. But you must stick to the principles of safe flight when you want your venture to take off.

The lifestyle business playbooks are designed to guide you step by step towards a business that works without having to make unoriginal mistakes. Behind each playbook, are painful crashes that destroyed businesses of the past. The playbooks might seem pretty simple now but their simplicity is the result of many failed attempts and human error.

The first thing you should know before you fly is if the weather is good enough. The same is true for business – you can't build a lifestyle business if the conditions aren't favourable. Fortunately for you, this is the greatest time in history to be an entrepreneur. The costs of launching a venture have fallen remarkably close to zero. We are blessed with abundant technology that opens us up to sharing ideas with the world, finding customers and recruiting collaborators. Free or cheap software has replaced expensive offices. Readily available data replaces guess work. AI gives you a tool that can be a lawyer, accountant, strategist, marketing consultant, analyst or creative director all at once, for free. It was unthinkable just a few decades ago that an unfunded teenager could build a multimillion-dollar business with customers all over the world – and now it's almost commonplace.

If you want to go far, you'll need a crew. They are out there just waiting for the right opportunity; the skilful and talented people you want to bring onto your team can be anywhere in the world and still add value. It used to be hard to find people. The right person had to live nearby your business and be available to work for a small business – this severely limited the scope of what an entrepreneur could build. Right now as you read this, there are some amazing humans going about their day in countries you've never been to and they are perfect collaborators. Unbeknownst to you or them your paths will soon cross, you'll find them online, they will join your team and you'll make magic together. You'll solve problems, deliver value and serve customers all over the world together before you even meet each other in person. They will have the skills you need and you will have the vision they are inspired by. You'll use the lifestyle business playbooks as a guide to channel your efforts into something fun and fulfilling.

All that's missing is your vitality. Your life-force energy, drive, determination, curiosity, grit, passion and ideas. The most wonderful people with the right skills are out there. All of the tools and technologies available are waiting to spring into action. They just need your direction. You are the organizing force, you are the director of the movie, the conductor of the orchestra. You are going to be the key person of influence who makes it happen.

Small teams have infinite leverage now. When you have a group of people who share a passion for solving a meaningful problem and they come together using the tools of entrepreneurship and the technology of our times, there's almost nothing they can't achieve. Small teams are going to radically transform the world in the coming years and the people who are part of these teams will achieve more in 3 years than most people do in 30. Having impact and having fun, freedom and fulfilment comes through the leverage of a small, passionate, aligned team. The playbooks are designed for you to bring out your best and bring out the best in others.

These six playbooks will take you through the key stages of getting your ideas to turn into a lifestyle business.

1. **The Apprenticeship:** You will find a mentor to work with and learn from. You'll add value to them and they will show you how it's done. You'll build self-awareness, commercial skills and gain access to more resources.

2. **The Side Hustle:** You will test your skills as an entrepreneur in a short, safe experiment. More important than

any money you make, this will build your confidence in readiness for bigger things.

3. **The Scout Team**: You and one other person will go and find an exciting opportunity. You'll discover if there is genuinely a market need and if it could probably be satisfied through a profitable business.

4. **The Firestarters**: A team of four will form and launch a new venture. You'll move fast in the right direction and spark something. It will be exhausting, resources will be tight and you'll be figuring it out as you go but you'll look back on this time fondly as the moment things really began to take off.

5. **The Core Team**: Your team will grow and you'll build a sustainable lifestyle business. You'll have fun, freedom, flexibility and financial success. Your team will be a tight unit that makes a big impact in the world. You'll all enjoy working together and you'll also get time to take breaks and travel. It will be magical. You'll be recognized in your industry as a key person of influence with a great team around you.

6. **The Performance Business** (maybe): You might choose to ramp things up and sell your business or exit the day-to-day operations. You might want to start something new. You might want to diversify your wealth. Maybe you want to pass on your business to new owners who have the ability to take it even further. You'll build a performance business that takes on a life of its own and becomes valuable in its own right.

As you explore the six playbooks, approach them with a beginner's mind. Regardless of how successful you are in business, explore the value in each playbook and how it could apply to your situation. If you are new to business, read all of them so you know how things unfold, and then study the first playbooks so you can begin applying them in the real world. If you are already advanced in business, consider that you may be the mentor an apprentice is looking for – it might be one of the most rewarding things you do. If you already have a business, you might want to pivot to something better and these playbooks can help you do that too.

The best approach is to read through all of the playbooks in order to understand how the journey unfolds. Then come back to the playbook that best represents your next move. Even if you already have an established business, you may want to pivot using the playbooks (for example, you could spin out a scout team to find a new opportunity).

These playbooks aren't designed to be read in a vacuum. You have powerful AI tools at your disposal to deep-dive into any details you want to better understand. AI can help you with job descriptions, standard operating procedures, marketing ideas or strategic business plans. These playbooks focus on the bigger context of how your ideas, curiosity, passion and drive is shaped into a lifestyle business.

AI is going to transform the nature of business in so many ways. I believe AI is going to shift power away from large corporations with thousands of workers towards small, dynamic teams. AI gives little teams awesome powers.

Every small business now has a lawyer, financial analyst, marketing manager, business advisor and customer service agents almost for free. It strikes me that some people who apply the playbooks to build a small lifestyle business of ten people could end up with a business that generates tens of millions in profit.

Even in an AI-enabled world, I believe the playbooks will be a reliable way to build something of value. Individuals, no matter how capable, rarely achieve anything great on their own. It's small dynamic teams of collaborators who shape the world. Never underestimate the power of a small group of people who are excited about the same things. This is how big things have always happened. It's also how humans most reliably experience joy.

CHAPTER 8

THE ENTREPRENEURIAL APPRENTICESHIP

ENTREPRENEURIAL APPRENTICESHIP PLAYBOOK

MISSION

Gain experience inside an existing lifestyle business working with IP, media, data, tech under the guidance of an experienced entrepreneur.

TEAM

Business Founder (mentor); Apprentice (you); Operational peer-group of 4–12 people.

OBJECTIVE

Experience the unfiltered realities of running a business and add value to an existing team. In the process, develop your commercial awareness, self-awareness and access to resources.

TIME FRAME

6–24 months.

KEY RESULTS

1. **Generate leads:** Get involved in a campaign that generates inbound sales opportunities (minimum 1,000 leads).

2. **Make sales:** Directly talk to customers, understand their criteria, handle objections and make sales (minimum 50 sales).

3. **Deliver value:** Work with paying customers to ensure they are happy enough to refer a friend (minimum 30 customers).

4. **Understand the numbers:** Get a clear understanding of the true revenues, costs and profits the business is making.

5. **Document your insights:** Keep a journal of your lessons and ideas for the future.

6. **Leave on good terms:** Ensure that when you leave this business, your relationship with the mentor is positive and they can genuinely say you added value.

TECHNIQUES

- Make a list of 30 small businesses you admire.
- Look through the finalists of small business awards.
- Notify people in your friendship group that you are looking for this opportunity.
- Offer to work for free for the right business.
- Complete sales and marketing-focused training.
- Capture video testimonials of happy customers for the business.
- Ask to be part of management meetings.
- Offer to build a financial forecast for the business.

MINDSET

- Eager to learn.
- Happy to be of service.
- Nothing is too big or too small of a task.

FAQS

Question	Answer
Where do I find a business to apprentice in?	Attend networking events for business owners. Look through small business awards for finalists and winners. Notify your friendship group you are looking for this sort of opportunity. Make a list of inspiring businesses you notice on social media and send direct messages to their founder.
What if I have zero experience?	Offer to complete a 90-day challenge for free or at a reduced rate. Start with basics like social media management, general admin, following up with old sales leads, checking in with existing customers.
Do I need to quit my job?	If possible start by taking some holiday leave or dropping back to part-time or alternative hours. Keep in mind you may not like entrepreneurship once you have an experience of it up close.
Tools and budget?	Basic tiers of Notion, Loom, Canva and ChatGPT will be useful enough during this challenge. You should be financially secure enough to withstand lower than normal income for at least 90 days.

I parked my car down the street for two reasons. I didn't want to be seen driving a bomb and it leaked oil. I walked up to the front door of the most impressive home I'd ever seen up close. The huge wooden door stood between me and a 30-minute face-to-face meeting with an experienced entrepreneur who was embarking on his latest venture. When it opened, Jon smiled at me and welcomed me in to his home office overlooking the pool at the centre of his designer home. We had scheduled 30 minutes but ended up talking for 3 hours and meeting his family. The deal was done, I would join his team along with two others who had signed on.

We worked around the kitchen table, the spare room and in the garage for the first few weeks organizing a launch campaign. There was a lot to be done – setting up bank accounts, naming the company, writing a direct mail sales letter inviting people to a launch event and calling through a list of contacts to secure sales appointments. At the end of each day we all sat on the back balcony nibbling on cheese and having a wine talking about how great this business was going to be.

When Jon needed to go to the airport I offered to drive him. He didn't care that my car was a bomb – he used the time in the car to teach me some sales skills with a set of role plays. When Jon needed to send out 1,000 letters, I stayed back folding, packing and addressing them. I was rewarded with a lesson on how he had written the sales letter following a specific formula.

I made endless sales calls. At least 70 times a day, I called someone new on my list. Jon told me to stand up and smile when I made sales calls – they can hear it in your voice when you're on your feet. It was true, I did get a better result when I was pacing and I got an even better result when I was holding a plastic sword. Then came the face-to-face sales meetings. They were relentless and came thick and fast once we launched. I did 12 hours of sales meetings a day for weeks on end; the first meeting was at 8 a.m. and the final meeting ended at 9 p.m.; I had 30 minutes for lunch and 30 minutes for dinner. One week I found myself doing sales meetings a 2-hour drive away. I set off at 6 a.m., got home at 11:30 p.m. I must have done thousands of sales meetings in my first year working with Jon and each week we found time to tweak and improve my approach.

By the end of year one we had moved office twice. We'd gone from the home into an office for 20 people and then into an inner city office for 60 people. I don't know exactly how much we had made in the first year but it must have been millions. I had made well over a million of sales personally and we had a dozen salespeople on the team by the end of the year. More than the money, the experience was life changing for me. I had been mentored by an entrepreneur on how it's really done. Before turning 20, I got to sit in on planning meetings, I saw the weekly numbers, I saw the reality of what goes on behind the shiny veneer, I experienced how much grit and how little glamour is required to get something to launch properly.

You just don't get that experience when you work for a big company. In a large corporate, most people have no idea how the sales are made or the leads get generated. It's impossible to tell what the whole business is involved in. You don't get invited into important meetings, you don't see the important numbers or get one-on-one training from the CEO. You might get asked to do menial tasks but you won't know why they are important; you certainly won't be driving the senior executives to the airport in your car that's falling apart while they role play sales calls with you. Almost none of what you learn in a big name company will help you as an entrepreneur.

To be an entrepreneur, first you need to see how a small business runs. You need to get behind the scenes and work with a small team of less than 12 people who are building a bike while they are riding it. If you currently work for a mega-corporation, government institution or you are new to small business, the first step to starting a business is not starting one – it's getting a job working as a direct report for an entrepreneur.

At the height of Paris Hilton's fame, her 22-year-old assistant was always in the background making sure every paparazzi encounter went off like a scheduled photo call and taking notes in meetings for product endorsements and TV show deals. The assistant was Kim Kardashian, and in the early 2000s, she learned every trick in the book on how to be a global superstar who was essentially famous for being famous. In 2007, when Kim launched season 1 of *Keeping Up with the Kardashians*, Paris sent her flowers – the apprentice had graduated to headline rival. Kim would go on to take Paris Hilton's playbooks for fame and fortune to new heights.

Seeing what goes on behind the scenes under the wing of a mentor is the first step to living the dream yourself. Apprenticing in the real world is far more powerful than studying something in books or classrooms.

What does YouTube, LinkedIn, Yelp, Yammer and OpenDoor have in common? They are all wildly successful Silicon Valley companies with a strong emphasis on technology. But there's something else. These companies are all started by people who were early employees of PayPal. Each of these companies was founded by people who had worked directly with Elon Musk and Peter Thiel when PayPal was still figuring out its offering and what to call itself. This group of people are now known as 'The PayPal Mafia' and they have a disproportionate impact on the big startups coming out of California. The PayPal Mafia have also been the early investors and advisors for Facebook, Airbnb, Shopify, Uber and Slack – each becoming worth billions of dollars.

Something special went on at PayPal in those early days and almost everyone who experienced it became a superstar entrepreneur and investor. The early team were immersed in a culture that produces fast-growth highly valuable technology companies. As a result, they were transformed to an extent that they all went off and replicated it in their own way. Not only did they continue with what they were taught while being mentored by Musk and Thiel, they also passed it on to their apprentices too. There's nothing like being up close and personal with a mentor, working on a growing business. No other type of learning comes close.

Here are your guidelines for getting an entrepreneurial apprenticeship:

- **No more than 12 people on the team:** your goal is to have direct contact with the founder of the business. Once a business goes past 12 people on the team, the amount of time the founder has to spend with each person drops through the floor. After 12 people, you'll find yourself talking to the second in command a lot more than the entrepreneur. Ideally (in a perfect world) you will be joining an experienced serial entrepreneur on their latest startup and you'll be getting in early. If you can be physically around the entrepreneur most days, even better. You can find these opportunities by looking at people who judge startup awards – they are often serial entrepreneurs who are starting new things themselves or they are connected to people who are. You can go to startup meetups; you'll be one of the few people looking to join a team so you'll be spoiled for choice. Search on LinkedIn, ask around your network for this specific opportunity, go scrolling on Instagram. Once you know what you are looking for, you'll start to notice they are everywhere. Reach out, be bold in sharing your enthusiasm to join the team and watch how quickly an entrepreneur will jump at the chance to have you on their fledgling team.

- **Marketing and sales focus:** entrepreneurship is a fancy word but it mostly translates to making sales by any means possible in the early days. You need to experience this harsh reality for yourself up close. If you can't stomach the sight of blood, you won't make it as a doctor and if you can't stomach doing a week of back-to-back sales meetings, you won't make it as an entrepreneur. Sales meetings don't just drop from the sky, it takes a special style of performance marketing to get warm leads flowing. If you've only ever worked with well-known brands you'll gasp at the way entrepreneurs need to hook attention and deliver a call to action in every marketing asset. You need to see it working and connect the dots that it's an essential part of launching. Startups can't leverage a brand or play the long game – it's scrappy, punchy and gritty at the coal face of entering a new market. Best you see it up close while you still have the option to go back to your old job.

- **Creating digital assets:** you can't learn the techniques for building a traditional business and then go on to create something that's digital, scalable, fun and ready for the post-AI world. You have to be around a founder who understands the power of content, code and automation. You want to sit in on meetings where you are discussing how AI-agents could be used to solve a problem. You want to be behind the scenes on a video shoot where the founder is pitching an idea to a camera ready to get viral reach on Instagram. You want to attend an event where the founder is speaking to an audience and enrolling them in an idea based on some new innovation or trend.

Ideally you'll have access to live dashboards, interesting meetings and a pool of digital resources to unlock growth.

- **Learning is more important than earning:** you're not doing an entrepreneurial apprenticeship to move up the income ladder. You are doing this to avoid losing money and making mistakes when it comes time to launch your own business. At least 10 of my ex-employees have gone on to build million-dollar businesses; they have all followed the playbooks they learned while working closely with me. When you work for a startup, expect to get paid a low base salary plus performance bonuses when you bring in money. The real value exchange is in what you learn – consider it to be a practical MBA that will earn you money after you graduate. Be very careful negotiating equity or options as part of your employment with a startup. Your goal is to leave on good terms and if you muddy the waters by holding shares it will either lock you in to stay longer than you need to or cause a rift when you try to sever the deal.

- **It doesn't matter exactly what they do:** you might know that your passion is skydiving or jive dancing and you suspect you might want to have a business that reflects this in the future. Your apprenticeship doesn't need to be based on your passion, it needs to give you specific commercial skills for launching and rapidly growing a startup. People who have apprenticed with me now run a wide variety of businesses I know nothing about – from saunas to music studios, air condition maintenance to aged care. These people who apprenticed with me now run very different businesses to mine but they applied the lessons and built confidence they picked up in my team. Choose your apprenticeship based on what you will learn about growth and business success, not based on what you eventually want to explore as your own business.

- **Be the best student:** the quality of mentoring is largely based on the quality of the student. You want to be the hardest worker on the team, you want to do things that aren't part of your job. Treat your mentor's business as if it were your own – when you spend money treat it as if it was coming out of your bank account, when you make money for the business celebrate it as if it's yours. In your spare time, read books, listen to podcasts, do research and find golden nuggets of information that help the business to succeed. When it comes time to move on, you will know how much you gained from your mentor and you want them to feel it was a fair trade where they got even more from you.

In the olden days, it was normal and expected that everyone did an apprenticeship to launch their career. From blacksmiths to scribes, the way to get going was to work as an apprentice to someone who was further along than you, to shadow them, receive mentoring from them and to learn the trade. Along the way, an apprentice would discover all of the tricks of the trade, where to get the supplies they need, how to solve tricky problems and how to make a decent living from their craft.

Somewhere along the way, we collectively shelved the idea of an apprenticeship and replaced it with a university degree. Instead of getting hands-on, real-world experience, young people go to university for a few years and learn from career academics. These academics have often themselves never left the academic world and are detached from reality in many ways.

Contrast this with someone who works in a small business. They are shoulder to shoulder with the founder of the business every day, they know how the business makes sales and how it delivers value to clients. They know who the main suppliers are and why they were selected. Often everyone in a startup knows the revenue numbers on a weekly basis; they know the biggest problem that needs solving and why it's important.

COACHING, MENTORING AND ACCELERATORS

The alternative to an apprenticeship is a mentor, a coach or an accelerator. If you are already in a business of your own, it's unlikely that you can also be an apprentice to another entrepreneur but you can get yourself the guidance you need.

A mentor is someone who has walked the path you are on and can show you how they did it. Ideally you want a mentor who you can meet with at least once a month and discuss what you're struggling with. This mentoring dynamic tends to be sustainable if they have a vested interest in your success – if they are a supplier to your business and your growth would result in bigger orders, if they are a shareholder in your company or if they are paid to be an advisor. Young entrepreneurs tend to get free mentoring easily from older entrepreneurs who want to keep their finger on the pulse with new approaches.

A business coach is a paid role, typically an experienced business person who has also studied coaching skills. This relationship mirrors the benefits of a mentor with a much cleaner financial arrangement. When you are paying a coach, it's easier to book in regular sessions at a time that suits you and to discuss the topics that you really want to explore. The right coach is someone you respect and admire and who also feels aligned to your aspirations.

The other option for entrepreneurs is to join an accelerator program with like-minded cohorts who are all going through the same process of development together. This is excellent because you get mentoring as well as peer-to-peer networking and access to resources. Be sure that the accelerator you join is focused on the outcomes you want – many are designed to create the next billion-dollar unicorn more than the next lifestyle business.

Note: we offer accelerators and coaches at www.dent.global.

If you are going to be an entrepreneur with a lifestyle business, you are going to want to do an apprenticeship or get a mentor. A lot of business can't be learned academically – you have to experience it.

Activity:

Look for all of the small business awards in your city that took place in the previous year. Read through the categories and the lists of finalists. Look for businesses that catch your eye that could be good to apprentice under the founder. Make a shortlist and reach out to the founders on their social media accounts with something like:

'I noticed you were a finalist in the XYZ Awards and it sparked me to do some research into your business. I'm really inspired by what you are working on and I'd be interested to join your team. I know you're a small business, so I'd be happy to do a trial period for free or to work on a specific outcome for you. I have a background doing [skills] and a passion for [topic]. Would you be up for having a quick call to discuss if there's anything I can do on your team that would add value?'

Alternatively, explore the coaching and accelerator options at www.dent.global

AI prompt (using a deep research feature):

'I live near [location] and I would like to work in a small dynamic business in this area. I want to work for an inspiring founder of a startup. I want to work in a business that has less than 12 full-time employees, hopefully a business that has entered for awards or been recognized in the media. I want to be around a business that is actively driving marketing, sales and product development and has a founder who is leading from the front. Search online and compile a list of 10 companies that I could approach. Also suggest 10 founder networking events or online groups where I might connect with someone who fits this description.'

CHAPTER 9

THE SIDE HUSTLE

Side Hustle Playbook

Mission

Without quitting your job, create a sideline campaign that generates at least one month of your typical income, within 90 days and you can easily shut it down once completed.

Team

Hustler (you); accountability buddy or collaborator (a friend).

Objective

Validate your entrepreneurial skills, build confidence and experience as an entrepreneur.

Time frame

Open and shut within 90 days.

KEY RESULTS

1. **Identify an opportunity:** Find a problem that can be solved and create a business opportunity and a plan to execute.

2. **Organize resources:** Set up the suppliers, tools and funding required to execute a campaign.

3. **Capture interest:** Find a low-cost entry to market, establish direct contact with potential customers and get them to signal interest.

4. **Make sales:** Generate sales exceeding your typical monthly income. Collect the money.

5. **Deliver value:** Ensure your customers are happy with what you delivered to them. Get testimonials or feedback whenever possible.

6. **Document your insights:** Keep a journal of your lessons and ideas for the future. Take photos and videos documenting the campaign.

7. **Wrap it up:** Conclude the challenge with no loose ends. All bills are paid, all money is collected and customers are happy.

TECHNIQUES

- Ideate on at least 10 business ideas before selecting one to execute.
- Talk plans through with a friend, collaborator or mentor figure.
- Use ChatGPT to explore the side hustle in depth and make detailed campaign plans.
- Role play sales scripts before talking to real prospects.

- Avoid long-term commitments (this is an open-and-shut campaign that lasts 90 days).
- Avoid trying to create the perfect plan. Only engage in a side hustle that you can fail at without harming your long-term prospects.

MINDSET

- Playful.
- Resourceful.
- Willing to look silly.

FAQs

Question	Answer
How do I pick a side hustle idea?	Start with the magic question from Shift 3: 'When did I do something special for a certain type of person and got a remarkable result and I can explain it step by step?' Package that result as a tiny product or service. Keep a journal of problems you notice. Your idea doesn't have to be something you want to do long term, it's just an open-and-shut campaign to test your business skills. Use ChatGPT to brainstorm 10 ideas. Avoid any side hustle that competes directly with your current employer.
Should I spend money on ads?	Leverage free channels first: social posts, direct messages, door-to-door sales, joint-venture partners. It's very easy to burn through thousands of dollars in ads without seeing a return.

Question	Answer
How can I collect payments and keep things legal?	Most people will happily pay you using PayPal, Stripe Express or Square. Ask Google or ChatGPT if you are required to register as a sole trader or complete any tax forms. Try to avoid setting up anything with a long-term commitment such as a company. This is a short-term test of your skills.
Time management tips?	Weekends and evenings are side hustle times – block it into your calendar. Get into alignment with your friends or partner that you are conducting a 90-day challenge and appreciate their support (or understanding).
Tools and budget?	Create a basic financial forecast for your side-hustle campaign and only proceed if you can afford a worst-case scenario – total failure. Use free or cheap tools like Google Docs, Canva and ScoreApp. Learn for free on YouTube or with AI tools. Do not pay for expensive support, coaching or training. Do not enter into long-term contracts that exceed the 90-day time frame.

I've just thrown 15 CDs and 10 T-shirts into the crowd, now the skateboard is held above my head; in front of me is a tightly packed nightclub full of teenagers, the DJ has swung the spotlight onto me as I give away prizes in the hottest nightclub in town. They're cheering, their sweaty faces are beaming up at me and I'm on a massive high. Later that night I count up the cash taken on the door and it's thousands of dollars. After expenses. I've just had my first taste of entrepreneurship and I'm hooked.

I was 18 years old when I moved out of home. I moved into a three-bedroom home with a group of five friends. My bedroom was the garage. I covered the concrete floor with second-hand carpet, bought a mattress for the floor and used suitcases for my clothes. I was seriously broke and urgently needed to cover rent. The first job I got was delivering pizzas for Pizza Hut, then I got a job as a barman in a wedding venue and then a door-to-door sales job on the weekends. Between these three jobs I had just enough money to live while also doing my first year of university.

I was out on my own, surviving on my wits and figuring out the realities of adulthood. I discovered that my local butcher had offcuts going cheap, the grocery store had a discounted 'ugly box' of veggies that didn't look the part and Pizza Hut let the drivers take home abandoned orders much to the delight of my housemates. Every Thursday night the top nightclub in town had a student party with heavily discounted drinks and we all got to let loose. Truth be told, it was an exciting time in my life.

At university, we were challenged to identify a market opportunity based on an unmet need and write a short business plan about it. One afternoon I got talking to some teenagers skateboarding on my street. They asked me what it was like going to nightclubs and I talked them through it – they couldn't wait to turn 18 and experience it for themselves. The penny dropped, these teens wanted something they couldn't do; this was an unmet need!

Rather than just writing about it, I began exploring the opportunity. I spoke to the nightclub and they were open to doing an underage alcohol-free Tuesday night if I was confident I could fill the venue. Then I spoke to the radio station and they agreed to feature the party on air if they could have the naming rights. I walked into a clothing shop and walked out with bags of cloths to give away as prizes, then a skateboarding shop gave me a new skateboard and the music shop gave me piles of CDs. McDonald's agreed to put up posters in their crew room and it was easy to hand fliers to teens in the mall. This was really happening.

From having the idea to running the party was less than 90 days. I'd managed to fit it all in around three jobs and my studies and suddenly I'd made more cash than all my jobs combined. Not to mention the fun of doing it. In the process I'd built my confidence in becoming an entrepreneur.

Side hustles are not about making money. They are about developing the skills and attitudes you'll need to build a business. They are the per-season games we play to warm up to going pro. A side hustle tests your commercial skills, gives you insights into your strengths and weaknesses and forces you to get resourceful – all essential for entrepreneurship at any scale.

Completing your mission to run a side hustle is an important step in becoming the type of person who can confidently build a lifestyle business. There are some rules I want you to follow to make the most of this challenge:

- **Don't quit your job:** It's called a side hustle for a reason – it's something you do on the side of what you are already doing. It needs to be something you can do in evenings, early mornings and weekends so that your current job doesn't suffer. A side hustle isn't likely to replace your stable income any time soon – it's a test run to see how you perform with your entrepreneurial skills.

- **Open and shut in 90 days:** A side hustle is a learning experience. If it drags on it ceases to become something you can learn from and morphs into something you are tied in to. There's a good chance that a side hustle isn't the right business opportunity for you long term. If you constrain yourself to an open-and-shut experiment that lasts no more than 90 days you will not overinvest, you won't overthink it and it forces you to have to move fast. At the end of 90 days, you can stop and review what you learned without the pressure to continue it any further.
- **Learning beats earning:** A side hustle doesn't need to be lucrative and it doesn't need to replace your income. It needs to make a profit, test your skills and give you valuable lessons. The real rerun on investment is the confidence you'll get from completing a challenge. A perfectly acceptable side hustle could make a few thousand dollars

but take you out of your comfort zone. Avoid side hustles that don't teach you much. Driving Uber isn't a side hustle, it's a part-time job; you're not learning how to be an entrepreneur taking rides from an app. Likewise, if you are a graphic designer in your day job, taking on a few private clients isn't a side hustle; you're not learning much doing more of what you know. You'd be far better off selling a box of special shower heads door to door, organizing a workshop or working with dentists to capture video testimonials for their customers. You're not doing this to supplement your income, you're doing this to become an entrepreneur with a lifestyle business.

- **This isn't a passion project:** A side hustle doesn't have to reflect your personal meaning of life. Your job is to identify an unmet need and fulfil it in exchange for money. Passion can come later – first you need the skills to execute. If you hold your side hustle to a standard where it needs to meet your emotional needs as well as be a successful campaign, you will blind yourself to obvious opportunities all around you. Purely and simply, evaluate the side hustle based on its merits as a way to test your entrepreneurial skills and build your confidence.

- **Don't ruin any relationships:** A side hustle is specifically *not* the time to burn your bridges. Do not create a side hustle that competes directly with your employer. Do not create a side hustle that causes your spouse to reconsider their vows. Do not borrow large amounts of money in the hope of paying it back when all goes to plan. All of these things have the potential to shatter your confidence as an entrepreneur and that is the very opposite of what this activity is designed for.

- **No big spending:** Do not engage in a side hustle that requires upfront setup costs that exceed an amount you can happily write off entirely. Find a way around spending money wherever you can. If your side hustle requires a professional camera, borrow one or hire it for a day as you need it. If a supplier wants you to buy 500 units of a product in order to get a discount, refuse to do it. It would be better to buy five of the products for retail cost and sell them at the same price just to see if you can sell them instead of committing to boxes of stock you may not be able to move.

- **Copy what works:** If you have seen someone execute a clever side hustle and you are drawn to try it out yourself, go for it. This challenge isn't about originality of ideas, it's about execution. Your goal is to have an experience of what it's like to roll up your entrepreneurial sleeves and get your hands dirty. Watching someone knock on a door and try to make a sale is nothing like doing it yourself for the first time. Reading about someone collecting a month's pay in an evening event barely fires off any dopamine but I can assure you when you do it yourself it will feel amazing. At this stage, there is nothing wrong with replicating something you've seen on YouTube or read about in a blog; just be sure it adheres to the other rules outlined above.

To get started on this challenge, come up with at least 10 side hustle ideas. Only when you have a full list, narrow it down to the best three. Evaluate your ideas based on the potential risks, the upside and the learning it will produce. Produce a simple spreadsheet of how you think this idea will perform – ask AI for some help with this forecast. Armed with three 'back-of-a-napkin' business plans, talk through the three ideas with people who are further along in business (this is part of the learning process). Say to them: 'I'm going to run a 90-day campaign to test my entrepreneurial skills, can I run my best three ideas past you and see which one you think is best? Don't worry, I won't blame you if it doesn't work out.' With some feedback from experienced entrepreneurs, select your best idea and get to work.

Don't overthink your execution. Start by sending some direct messages, knock on some doors, make calls and set up some sales meetings. Entrepreneurship is largely about making sales in the early days so do not avoid it. Pitch, pitch, pitch your side hustle to anyone who will listen. Trust that one thing will lead to the next thing so long as you are making contact with the market. The big mistake is 'playing dress-ups' as an entrepreneur. This is where you talk to suppliers, rent a desk in a co-working space, design a logo, print a hoodie or fuss over a website. I call all of this 'ABS Breaking' and it stands for doing 'anything but sales'.

You probably don't need a logo, a website, a desk or a uniform – you need sales. Unless something is directly linked to making sales, be very sceptical of it. I have knocked on thousands of doors and I didn't have a branded uniform – just a clipboard, a pen and an order form. Rather than a website, set up a landing page for people to respond to an offer (you can do this cheaply and easily on ScoreApp). Even running a webinar on Zoom lets you create a registration page. Leverage existing platforms that allow you to sell things rather than spending weeks building your own site. Make sales fast – it's the only way to win with a side hustle.

At the end of 90 days, compile your learning. What were you afraid to do but then it turned out to be fine? What did you suck at? What were you surprisingly great at? What did you enjoy the most? What would you have done differently? How much did you spend? How much did you make? Write up a two-page debrief, include photos and videos that you took along the way. Most importantly celebrate the experience regardless of the financial result. Head out to a nice restaurant with a few friends, present them with your report and share what you learned from the experience and celebrate the fact you completed a side hustle. Let it feel good – not because you've arrived at your destination but because you are now on the path.

In my early days as an entrepreneur, I ran nightclub parties, sold roses door to door for Valentine's Day and improved marketing materials for an established business. All of these side hustles laid the foundations for building a multimillion-dollar business in my early twenties. To be honest, the feeling I got from selling 100 roses door to door and making $360 profit was even better than the feeling I got last time I raised $1 million of funding for a tech startup. Enjoy these early experiences – you will remember them fondly long after you've become an established entrepreneur with millions in the bank.

Activity:

Start a note in your phone (or a journal if you prefer) for keeping track of entrepreneurial ideas or opportunities you notice. Evaluate each idea based on your passion, your ability to solve a meaningful problem and the likelihood that a lot of people would happily pay for it. No idea is too big or small to write down. You might notice a dirty car on your street – write down the idea of offering to wash the car for the owner. You might notice your bank's app is clunky – write down the idea to redevelop their software systems. The goal is to get better at spotting opportunities and being able to describe in writing why you think it would be a good idea for you or not.

AI prompt:

'Help me to brainstorm 10 ideas for me to try as an entrepreneurial side hustle. I want to do something that I can start and finish within 90 days. I want it to carry a low financial or reputation risk. This venture should optimize for learning about business and building my confidence in marketing and sales. Ask me questions first to better understand what kind of idea would be appropriate. Then give me 10 ideas to chose from. When I select an idea from the list, guide me through the step-by-step approach to launching this side hustle venture and achieving success in under 90 days'.

CHAPTER 10

THE SCOUT TEAM

Scout Team Playbook

Mission

Scout a potential long-term lifestyle business opportunity that has the potential to generate $1 million in annual sales.

Team

Sales scout; delivery scout; mentor.

Objective

Through direct contact with the market, research and data analysis you will discover the opportunity that is right for you to commit to long term.

Key results

1. Generate **10 business ideas.** Using the criteria of passion, problem and payment, narrow down to 1–3 ideas to scout.
2. Capture **150 expressions of interest** (EOIs) via cold-outreach, affiliate partners and micro-ads.

3. Complete **30 deep-dive discovery calls** and log insights in a spreadsheet.

4. Draft a **financial forecast** proving ≥ 50% gross margin is possible after IP, media and technology are in place.

5. Produce an **Ideal Customer Persona canvas** (pains, prizes, obstacles, budget).

6. Produce basic **marketing assets** including a pitch deck, landing page, email/direct-message campaigns, explainer video.

7. Track LAPS data and present a **Go/Kill/Pivot** report to a mentor for feedback.

TECHNIQUES

- Launch a waiting list campaign.
- Create an online discussion group.
- Run introduction webinars.
- Launch an online needs assessment.
- Aim for face-to-face sales meetings (or at least on video call).
- Present prospects with brochures and materials.
- Ask customers 'On a scale of 1–10, how likely are you to recommend this offer to someone? Why did you select that number?' and track their responses.
- Document and improve your CAOS – concept, audience, offer, sales – process.

MINDSET

- Deeply curious.
- Willing to explore.
- Happy to get hands dirty.

FAQs

Question	Answer
How do we recruit scouts?	Ask around your friendship groups and colleagues, post on social media (especially in entrepreneur discussion groups), attend startup networking events.
What's the cheapest way to get 150 EOIs?	Create a landing page for registering interest (e.g., a waiting list, webinar registration) and send direct messages (text or voice) to at least 100 people per day on social media until you hit 150 who opt in. Additionally post relevant content every day on social media, join groups and attend existing events where your potential ICPs will be.
Should I set up a CRM?	A shared Google Sheet with status columns is fine until you surpass 1,000 leads.
When do we 'kill' an idea?	If less than 10% of discovery calls show genuine interest, urgency and ability to pay, you will want to seriously consider archiving the idea and move on to your next approach (e.g., you deliver a sales presentation to 30 people and less than 3 are willing to commit to becoming customers).

The kids are in the back seat of the car making noise, my wife is driving us to a local park and I'm glued to my phone in the passenger seat. Cut, paste, send. Cut, paste, send. Cut, paste, send. I'm firing off direct messages on Instagram and LinkedIn. I've committed myself to exploring a new business idea and I'm hustling every spare minute to test the market. Here's the message I'm sending:

> *Hi, a few years ago I launched a marketing campaign that massively outperformed and flooded us with perfect clients. It all centred on an online assessment we launched. It's probably one of the best campaigns I've run and I've tried a lot of things. I'm going to run a Zoom workshop on how I did this and talk you through the step-by-step blueprint. There's no big sales pitch, I'm just exploring if this is something that more businesses could benefit from. If you want to attend, let me know and I'll send you the Zoom link.*

Across the course of the month I sent 100–200 messages a day and ran a Zoom call every week with about 50 people each time. On the Zoom call I present people with my case study, showcase the basic outline of the software we are building and then open up for questions. I tell people that when we launch, it will cost $1,000 to set up and then $50 per month to subscribe and give people the chance to register for the beta group access as soon as the product is ready.

The questions people ask are invaluable to my co-founder Steven Oddy and I. These potential customers are asking questions we hadn't even thought of and it's sparking ideas for features we want to build into our new venture ScoreApp. At the end of the month we've presented our initial pitch to almost 200 potential customers and about 60 have joined the waiting list. These numbers are acceptable to move to the next stage of building this business but had they been terrible, we would have killed this idea off before spending any serious time or money on it.

Behind the scenes, Steven is building a basic version of the software platform; just enough for us to get a sense of the technical challenges we might face if we really lean in to this. We've also signed up six clients who have agreed for us to build them something similar from scratch using Word-Press so we can be hands-on with real customers and see exactly what they want.

The focus at this point is to get a true indication if people want to pay for this and if we give them what they want while still making a profit. In addition to this, we're getting a sense as to how much fun this business might be; are we feeling excited about committing further to this venture or does it feel like a drag?

Fast, cheap experiments are our focus. We are like scientists, gathering data to validate or disprove our hypothesis. We don't have an office, we don't have a company or a bank account, there's no logo and no website. We really don't need any of that stuff yet in order to conduct our experiments.

THE CAOS METHOD

The scout team have four things to explore:

- Concept – is the idea worth pursuing?
- Audience – do we have the ability to get attention from the right people?

- Offer – can we present the right people with a product or service they want?
- Sales – do we have the ability to get sales flowing at an allowable cost?

CONCEPT

A great concept is one that creates a sense of alignment. Alignment is that feeling you get when something is right for you. You feel drawn to it, compelled to act and the creative juices naturally flow. It doesn't feel like something you should do, or something you're drawn to because it's easy money. It's something you feel like you must do even if it's hard to do. It feels almost destined and like your personal story has led you to this point. It also feels like very few other people would be right for this; this is something that is meant for you.

To get a great idea, it's wise to have plenty to choose from. You want to keep a journal or a note in your phone and try to uncover ten ideas that might be right for you. When you have ten, call a meeting with some friends, mentors or advisors and run them through your ideas to see which one they think is best for you and why. The criteria you want to explore is your levels of passion for the idea, the size of the problem that you are solving and the amount of money people would pay to solve it. Some ideas score high on passion but aren't solving a big problem that people will pay for. Other ideas might look lucrative but you can't muster the passion. You need an idea that balances these elements even if you have to make a compromise.

A fair way to evaluate your ideas is to score them on a scale of 1 to 10 for each category – passion, problem, payment. You're looking for an idea that scores above a 21 overall, which means it's at least a 7 out of 10 on all three criteria. The idea also has to tick the boxes that it will eventually become a lifestyle business. It can't tether you to one location. It can't always be centred on you selling your time and skills for money to one person at a time. It needs to have the potential to be mostly grown through digital, scalable assets and it should seem reasonable that it could earn great profit. It's not easy to find an idea that ticks these boxes, which is why it's worth exploring more deeply. Even if it takes you an extra three months to start, finding the right concept for you to develop is worth it.

When you have selected your concept, craft an elevator pitch so you can tell people about it. Your elevator pitch will tell people:

Name: *The name of this business or product.*

Same: *What it's similar to so people understand it.*

Fame: *What makes it different or special.*

Pain: *What is the problem are you solving.*

Aim: *What you are hoping to achieve in the next few months.*

Game: *What's the bigger picture for this if it succeeds.*

For example: 'I'm launching BookMagic.ai (name). It's software that gets people to write a book better and faster than they could with Microsoft Word (same). I've written several books and my co-founder has worked in publishing for decades, working closely with thousands of first-time authors (fame). About 50% of adults want to write a book but less than 2% of people currently do it (pain). We've discovered a way of getting AI to guide people through a proven writing process that used to cost a fortune and only be available to the best authors and we will be launching a beta group of 300 authors who will each use the AI-powered software to write a book (aim). If this succeeds we want to roll this out to millions of adults who want to write a book in their lifetime but don't know where to start (game).'

AUDIENCE

When you have a concept, your next job is to capture the attention of your potential buyers. This involves identifying the right person who will be your best ideal customer persona and then hooking their attention with a simple marketing campaign to garner signalled interest from them.

You must ask yourself the question 'who will get the most value from this concept?' and formalize this hypothesis into an ideal customer persona document. Every concept will resonate with a certain type of person more than others. You want to choose a type of person who has money to throw at their problems. They either spend money already and you can deliver something better, faster or cheaper than what they've got. Alternatively they have disposable income or surplus profit they can allocate to something new. As a general rule, sell to people in the top 10% of earners or to businesses with existing revenue in the top 10% of the industry.

When you have identified your ideal customer persona, your next task is to set up a campaign designed to capture signals of interest. This typically takes the form of a landing page for a:

- **Waiting list**: A web page that allows people to register their interest in an offer that is coming in the future. For example: 'New AI software for authors is coming soon. It allows you to write a book better and faster. Join the waiting list to get early access when it goes live.'

- **Discussion group**: This allows people to request access to a private online group for people who are discussing a topic of interest. For example: 'Ever thought of writing a book? Join the discussion with writing experts, publishers and aspiring authors. Request access to the private WhatsApp group.'

- **Assessment**: This is an online self-assessment to see if someone is ready or suitable to achieve an outcome. For example: 'Are you ready to write a book? Answer 12 questions to see if your book idea will get published and fly off the shelves.'

- **Workshop**: This is an online workshop that teaches the process to achieving something an ideal customer wants to achieve. For example: 'How to write a book in under 90 days – join expert writing coach and book publisher to discover how to get your book out of your head and onto Amazon fast.'

Note: All four of these campaigns can easily be set up with ScoreApp, using the templates provided. You can start with a free account at ScoreApp.com. When setting up your landing page be sure to hook people's attention with a compelling headline, give them at least three benefits for engaging, share what makes you credible and give them a clear action step.

THE 150-TEST

To test your audience, you must get 150+ people to engage with your first audience building campaign. You can e-mail or message people, post on social media, go networking in the real world or even run some ads (if you can afford to lose the money). However you do it, you need to prove you can get 150 to fill in a form. If you can't get people to fill in a form for free, it's unlikely you will get them to part with their money. The other purpose of this activity is to discover more about your target customer. When they join a waiting list, fill in an assessment, register for a workshop or enter a discussion group make sure they answer a few questions first. Ask them:

Which best describes your current situation?

Which best describes your most desired outcome?

What has held you back or frustrated you in achieving this outcome?

What have you previously tried that didn't work?

What budget would you happily spend if you felt confident in getting your desired result?

Is there anything else you want me to know?

The answers to these questions will allow you to fine-tune your marketing and your offer.

OFFER

When 150+ people have signalled their interest in your concept by filling in a form, it's time to test your offer. A concept is a general description of what your business is about, an offer is a specific description of what a customer can buy. It covers exactly what they get and how much it costs.

Construct multiple offers – a gold, silver and bronze version of what you have in mind. Stretch your thinking and imagine what your offer would be if your customer was a multimillionaire who just wanted to throw money at their problems and get big things done fast. Then imagine your buyer is in a remote, distant city on the other side of the world and they want to buy from your business and get an outcome wherever they are. Explore what your solution would be if it had to be software, or a training programme, or a physical bundle of products, or if it had to be highly entertaining.

Customers are not mind readers – far from it. Over half the human brain is used for visual processing so it is imperative that you communicate every offer visually. This takes the form of a slide deck, landing page or brochure. You want to show people images that represent the problem, solution and typical buyer. You want clear text, images and diagrams. Include written testimonials, charts, graphs, research, statistics, cartoons, renderings, illustrations and anything else that shows people the value of what you do. Creating these documents won't only provide clarity for your customers, the process is brilliant for clarifying your thinking too. You want to end up with three clear options to present to people to see which they gravitate to.

The 30-Test

When you are armed with your documents, your next challenge is to present your offer to 30 people in a live environment. This would ideally be one-on-one, in-person sales meetings so you can really see people reacting to everything you show them. Alternatively you can do group presentations or online video-meetings if necessary.

Reach out to the people on your list of 150 and ask if they'd be willing to be one of the first to see what you are developing. Tell them their feedback will help shape your offer and they will be the first in line to see the finished version when it's ready.

During the meetings, ask people about their current situation and what they are hoping to achieve. Explore their current frustrations and what they have previously tried that didn't work. Present them with your solution and how you have developed it. Make sure they understand your credibility and the insights you have into the topic. Also share your underlying purpose for creating this offer beyond making money – tell them why this offer really matters to you. When they understand the offer, ask them if it's ok to discuss the pricing plans. Present them with the three options you have developed and ask them which, if any, they would be most interested in going ahead with. After asking this question, stay silent and let them think and respond.

They know the offer isn't ready yet so the next question will throw them off a bit. Ask them: 'would you like to put down a deposit today to secure this offer, at a discounted price when we launch?' The real reason you ask this question is to uncover any hidden resistance they have but haven't told you about. People will give you polite responses when buying something that is theoretical but when you are asking for money, they'll give you real talk. If they are unwilling to put down a deposit, probe a little further to find the real resistance they didn't want to share earlier.

At a minimum you want 3 out of 30 people to agree to placing a deposit. Ideally you want more than 6 out of 30 – if that happens you're onto a real winner.

SALES

The lifeblood of every startup is the sales process. It doesn't have to be sophisticated or automated. I have made sales over the phone using scraps of paper to write down credit card details. I've called through business cards I had stored in an old shoe box. I've used basic spreadsheets as a CRM system for well over a thousand people in a sales pipeline. What's non-negotiable is that you can generate leads, book appointments, present your offer and close sales in a reliable way. We call this LAPS (leads, appointments, presentations and sales).

The goal of the scout team is to discover the basic LAPS numbers. How much does it cost to generate a warm lead using ads? Or how many cold messages do we need to send in order to get someone to say they are interested? How many leads are required in order to get an appointment booked into the diary? How many appointments do we have to present in order to get a sale? What is the total cost of time, effort and money to make a sale? How much money is a typical sale?

We're getting some initial numbers that marketing teams will later obsess over and optimize – the cost per lead (CPL), lead to conversion rate (CVR), cost to acquire a customer (CAC) and the projected lifetime value of a client (LTV). We need these numbers to be in the ballpark of a business that could sustain itself financially. If only one in 100 leads buy something and it costs $12 to generate a lead and the average lifetime value of a customer is $500, what should you do? Counterintuitively, it's not as bad as it seems. Yes, it cost $1,200 to generate a $500 sale and on the surface this doesn't seem like a good business but $12 per lead is pretty low in many industries. If we can figure out how to close another 3 sales per 100 and we can get the LTV up to $750 then we can spend $1,200 and make $3,000. It would be well worth exploring what it would take to get to those numbers.

The scout team should conduct sales experiments to test several approaches and the numbers they produce. With these numbers it will be possible to forecast if this idea could really become a business. When you have a clear understanding that you can sell something and deliver it profitably, it's time to grow the team and really start a fire burning!

Activity:
Come up with 2–10 ideas for businesses or products you want to launch. Use ScoreApp.com to set up a waiting list campaign (use the templates provided in a free account). For each idea, promote the waiting list by sending 150 direct messages to people who might be

suitable buyers and track how many people respond by joining the waiting list. When people join the waiting list, be sure to ask them 5–10 questions that help you to collect the data you need to improve your idea and price the offer.

Note: Even if you have an established business, this activity will help you to identify an innovation, feature or new product you can develop.

AI prompt:

'I'm exploring starting a new business. I want it to tick three boxes – something I am passionate about, something that solves a meaningful problem and something that targets an ideal customer persona who is willing to pay a premium for added value. I want you to ask me several questions to help me brainstorm the right business for me. Tell me the strengths and weaknesses of each idea and why it would or wouldn't be a good founder fit for me. After the questions are answered, I want you to produce an elevator pitch using a framework like business name, same, fame, pain, aim and bigger game. Then I want to produce a detailed description of my ideal customer persona. Then I want to create a detailed offer for them in a gold, silver and bronze version. Act as a business startup advisor like Daniel Priestley the entrepreneur and author.'

CHAPTER 11

THE FIRESTARTERS

Firestarter Team Playbook (Launch Squad)

Mission

Officially launch the business and generate sufficient revenue to justify the assumptions on the financial forecast. Prove that you can manufacture demand predictably.

Team

Associate key person of influence (figurehead); sales lead; delivery lead; operational support.

Objective

Execute a powerful launch campaign and prepare for growth.

Time to Complete

6–18 months.

KEY RESULTS

1. Generate sufficient **inbound leads** over a prolonged period.

2. Establish **sales conversion metrics** in line with an acceptable financial forecast.

3. Improve your average cost per lead (CPL), average cost to acquire a customer (CAC) and average lifetime value of a customer (LTV).

4. Secure **20 public video testimonials** and case-study consent forms.

5. Achieve an average **experience score** of at least 8 out 10.

6. **Document** best practices, in-house playbooks and dashboard metrics. Prepare to recruit new members of the team.

7. Create a **financial forecast** based on actual results. Track ongoing performance against the forecast (pay close attention to cash at bank).

TECHNIQUES

- Morning team huddle (30–60 mins) to establish highest value activities. Afternoon debrief (15 mins) for accountability.

- Set up a team discussion group, shared files, credit card and performance dashboard.

- Run launch events with your associate key person of influence (AKPI), leverage their reputation in sales and marketing activities.

- Promote a product for prospects that naturally leads to core product sales.
- Test small paid advertising campaigns with the intention of scaling up ad spend.
- Engage affiliates or joint-venture marketing partners.
- Stick to a 'payment first then delivery' policy.

FAQs

Question	Answer
Where do we find an AKPI?	Look for authors, speakers or social media influencers. Alternatively, look for people who have achieved an outstanding level of success whom your ICP will admire. Make a list of at least 30 suitable candidates and reach out to them for a call or a meeting to discuss the prospect of them being a speaker, non-executive director, advisor or co-founder to the business. Expect to pay their rates. Many of these people are paid extremely well for speaking or consulting gigs. Do not expect them to work for free. Instead negotiate small blocks of their time and agree favourable payment terms.
Funding the ad spend?	Pre-sell initial customers who pay up front and allocate a portion of sales revenue to ads. Research free ad credit available for startups. With confidence, utilize credit cards at a level of low risk.

Question	Answer
Tools and budget?	Utilize basic monthly subscriptions to products like Zoom for webinars, a basic CRM like Pipedrive, ScoreApp for lead generation, Google docs, MailChimp or AWS simple e-mail service and LinkedIn Premium. Use premium ChatGPT to support productivity (including exploring your tech stack options). Utilize remote contractors where necessary from marketplaces like UpWork (e.g., for preparing a financial forecast).
What is a typical marketing to sales conversion pipeline?	For a services business – 100 warm leads, 20 booked appointments, 14 sales presentations, 2 sales. For a software business – 100 warm leads, 30 free trials, 3 paid accounts. Note: Marketing to sales pipelines vary considerably, the important thing is that your sales conversions will fit within an acceptable financial forecast.

I'd never been above the equator. As I rode the train from Heathrow Airport into London, I was a bit shocked to see the terraced homes and chimneys. I'm not sure what I was expecting but growing up in a beach-side town in Australia didn't expose me to this sort of architecture. I wasn't there on holiday though – I was there to launch a business and I had very limited funds to do so.

In the first few weeks, I assembled my team. I had Mike who was raring to make sales, Joey was my executive assistant who could do almost any general task in her sleep. I also had a mentor, Thomas Power, who was a well-known founder at the heart of an entrepreneur ecosystem. Thomas agreed to meet me and open some doors for me in London.

My first move in London was to host a dinner party for potential marketing partners. Instead of spending money on ads, I wanted to get people who had email lists to promote my business in exchange for a commission. Through Thomas, I was able to invite 30 people to a private dining experience. After we ate I stood up, introduced myself and explained that my new business, Triumphant Events, was launching soon. I asked if each person would be willing to have a meeting to discuss how we could partner together.

The following two weeks I had over 20 one-on-one meetings and secured agreements with people to support our launch campaign. On the day of the launch, the e-mails all went out and 800 people booked into our big launch events in London, Birmingham and Manchester.

These events were a huge hit and generated over a million in new sales. The momentum continued and by the end of the first six months we were uptown four million in sales revenue. Mike was making sales and had recruited more salespeople. Joey was organizing everything and had recruited an event manager and a bookkeeper. I had started to get a good reputation of my own in London and could secure meetings without going through Thomas. People had said it would be hard to break into London – they reminded me that barely 5% of businesses hit a million of revenue in the UK – but here we were blasting through this milestone in our first few months. I had achieved this starting with a suitcase and a credit card!

It's remarkable what a small team can do these days. A few passionate people, aligned to a clear set of goals can make more impact today than at any other time in history. Your firestarter team is going to get your business up and running. You won't be doing things perfectly – you'll be focused on doing a few things well and staying directionally correct. The business will eventually run on refined systems and beautifully produced assets, but that comes later. This stage of the journey is messy – you are going to kick the door off the hinges, you'll move fast and break things, you'll act first and ask for forgiveness later. It's impossible to steer a parked car – your job is to create some movement.

There are four roles you'll need to have on your firestarter team: association key person of influence, sales lead, delivery lead and operational support.

1. **Associate key person of influence (AKPI):** This person isn't on your team day to day but their presence will be felt in almost every conversation. They won't be attending your team meetings but they will open doors for you, give you a steer in the right direction and lend you their credibility. This person is already known, liked and trusted in their industry. They have probably written a book, they have been around for 20+ years building their reputation, they probably get invited to speak and they will likely have over 10,000 followers on social media.

Why will this person work with your firestarting team? They will do it because it's a very leveraged way to make money and have fun. You are going to present them with a great deal that works for them – with minimal effort and no risk, they'll earn a lot and enjoy the process.

Some example deals that I have either done myself or seen implemented are:

- **Speaker/consulting fees:** The AKPI agrees to be a speaker at a launch event and subsequent events. For a few hours of their time, they earn what most people get paid in a month. Your business gets to use their name and profile throughout the whole campaign. It's often built into the agreement that they will have several meetings before each event and this is your chance to ask them key questions and show them your progress – treat every meeting with them as a critical moment. When they like what they are seeing, they can't help themselves but to make introductions or give valuable advice.

- **A cut of sales:** You can do a deal where the AKPI receives a percentage of every sale your business makes for an agreed period of time. My first business paid 5% of every sale to our AKPI. In exchange, we got valuable advice and the explicit use of his personal brand association. When the AKPI is receiving a cut of revenue, they are incentivized to make sure your team are performing. They might see the value in doing a sales training session with you and your team, they will almost certainly put you in touch with a strategic partner or bring you into a high-level meeting they are having. Remember that your AKPI is busy and has multiple deals on the go. Just because they have a cut of revenue doesn't mean you will always be on the top of their mind, it's your job to work the partnership not theirs.

- **An equity stake:** This is an option but it's the least proffered for all involved. An AKPI won't really want to own a small piece of your lifestyle business because they will know from experience that it won't produce much for them. A lifestyle business by definition isn't being built to sell for billions and a minority stake has no real power to enforce dividend payments or a buyout – unless you deliberately build it into your shareholders' agreement. If you do this, you'll eventually have a small shareholder who can push for decisions you might not want to make. With that said, if you believe in the value of a long-term, aligned partnership and the equity deal locks it in place, it's worth exploring.

2. **Sales lead:** The next role is sales and marketing, responsible for driving LAPS (leads, appointments, presentations and sales) through the business week on week. This is probably going to be the founder of the business. For most startups, founder-led sales is the only way to get going because great salespeople are too expensive to hire and tend to take control of a new business if they are aware they control the money.

It is still too early to build a sophisticated sales and marketing engine. You must not be afraid to grind for your sales in the early days. It's not unheard of to send hundreds of direct messages on social media each day and to do endless face-to-face meetings with potential customers. Your goal is to get close to your customers not to use a system to get distance from them. I have driven four hours to attend a meeting with potential clients – for a digital product. It's not the money I want, it's the deeper understanding of what makes them tick.

Part of this role is taking responsibility for creating marketing and sales assets. In addition to selling to potential customers, this person is going to be capturing ideas for marketing copy, ads, brochures, social media content and the like. While juggling a sales pipeline, you'll also be talking to suppliers to make landing pages, build a diagnostic quiz, edit videos, design slide decks, mock up product designs and anything else you need to reach more people.

3. **Delivery lead:** This role is focused on making customers happy. There are two parts to this role, the first is the short-term job of delivering upon whatever the sales lead promised. This can be tricky when each client was promised something slightly (or wildly) different. As infuriating as it may be in the moment, remember that the sales lead is still feeling around in the dark trying to discover what people want. They aren't deliberately being a nuisance for the fun of it – part of the process is to try things. The second part of this role is to spot the themes and formalize elements of the offer into a more scalable product.

You're going to be building some basic workbooks, posters and maybe even a customer portal. You'll use off-the-shelf solutions at this stage – you don't have the resources to custom build anything yet. Your early customers don't expect you to have all the bells and whistles in place. They know it's early days and they are excited to be one of the first customers to go on the journey with you. At some point you are going to build more comprehensive assets, so any time you can collect something useful for the future you'll store it away safely – a video testimonial, an idea for a software platform, a powerful feature customers would love, an advanced AI integration, a script that will be useful for your customer success agents you will hire one day soon.

This role will be juggling the needs of clients today with the desire to build something that scales. Early-stage businesses are hard because you are running a marathon while also building a bike. Despite being stretched and wishing you had time to focus on one thing, it is this strange mix of hands-on customer delivery with systems thinking that will make your offer unique in the market. Bigger businesses almost never get their hands dirty like this. Their product team rarely meet real customers in the flesh, their customer success agents aren't in constant communication with the developers. Park the frustration and embrace the chaos as a rare and beautiful time in your career to develop something that is really connected to what customers are crying out for.

4. **Operational support:** This role is for a high-agency generalist. Like a Swiss Army knife, this person can do 25 things but isn't a specialist in any of them. Nothing is beneath them and nothing is too grand. They can do data entry, logistics, scheduling, social media updates, appointment setting, event management, customer service and basic accounting. This person has probably worked in hospitality like a cafe, restaurant, nightclub or small hotel or maybe they grew up in a small business family. In those environments, you're always juggling multiple things, all of them are urgent, and you just roll up your sleeves and make it all happen.

They could spend the morning at a printing business collecting boxes of brochures; the afternoon is spent calling through a list of event attendees confirming their dietary requirements while also responding to social media messages. Then it's a quick shower before heading over to the

venue to set up the audiovisual equipment and then wel-
coming guests to a private dinner and launch presentation.
To top it all off, they also post several short videos on social
media about how the day went and make sure all the receipts
get entered into the accounting software.

This person is not precious. Their last job wasn't for
a big corporation. They've never called in an information
technology manager to set up a projector or contacted a HR
person to check if the overtime they did last month can be
transferred to additional annual holidays. They don't spend
any time looking at what's in the job description – their job
description is 'whatever needs to be done right now to make
it through this week'.

With your firestarter team in place, there are two types
of products you need to promote: the product for prospects
and the core offer.

1. **Product for prospects:** The product for prospects is
   a pre-product that warms people up to doing business
   with you. It is far more powerful to promote a product
   for prospects instead of the core offer. The core offer
   requires a relatively bigger commitment of effort and
   money and if people don't know your business, they're
   unlikely to make that commitment. A product for prospects requires no money, a small amount of effort and the
   willingness to share some data. My first company, Triumphant Events, specialized in running introduction events.
   We worked with financial planners, franchises, training
   providers and software providers to run free workshops

that educated people about the issues that related to each business. It is much easier to get people to attend a free two-hour workshop about economic trends, than to sign up with a financial planner you don't know.

Every business I have run since, has launched by promoting a product for prospects first. The three most reliable examples are:

- **Introduction workshop/event:** A free 1–2 hour presentation that covers the key topics relating to what you do. For example: 'How to get fit over 50 – Register for the free workshop'.
- **Online assessment:** A free online quiz that gives people an immediate insight into something they want to improve. For example: 'Are you ready to get fit over 50? Answer two questions and find out which strategy suits you best'.
- **Common interest discussion group:** An online group that people can join to discuss their journey and get questions answered. For example: 'Ready to get fit over 50? Join the WhatsApp daily motivation group for free.'

2. **Core offer (in two versions):** The core offer is the main thing your business does but the way you see your core offer is vastly different to the way your customer sees it. You will see the inputs and components of what you do, while the customer sees it as a path of least resistance for them to get an outcome they want. A simple example is a fitness trainer sees what they do as delivering training

sessions in the gym to ensure the customer follows good form and applies best practices. The person who buys fitness training sessions is buying what they believe to be their best pathway towards looking or feeling better. If the customer could wave a magic wand and get the result, they would prefer that option.

It is important for you to learn how to present what you do in the language of the customer. Customers need to see slide-decks, brochures or landing pages in order to understand fully what you offer. They need you to spell out for them what they get, the outcomes they can expect to see and what it will cost them. They want to know if there are risks and how those risks are reduced. They want to see the results visually laid out for them and the process for getting these results.

They also want at least two options to choose from. You should present people with a choice between the 'gold or silver package' – much better than choosing to buy or not buy. You can package in as many things as you like with what you do. A restaurant buys champagne and adds it to the bill – they don't have to own the vineyard in order to offer you a glass of bubbles, they just package it in. Your customers want you to package in more stuff to make their life easier. A fitness trainer should have a gold package that includes fitness clothing, a photo shoot, a subscription to a food tracking app and some home gym equipment. All of this stuff already exists but when bundled in, adds huge value to a customer.

You have a team, a product for prospects and a core offer. Now you must focus on a few key activities:

- **Daily huddle and debrief:** Every morning, you get together for a short, sharp meeting to coordinate your efforts to drive sales and delight customers. If you all work remotely, you can do this on a video call but it's wise to get the team in the same room as often as possible to set the pace and chemistry.

- **Weekly LAPS:** Your most important activity is to establish a rhythm of generating leads, booking sales appointments, delivering sales presentations and following up in order to close sales. Your leads will come by promoting your products for prospects. Everyone who registers for an event, takes the assessment or joins the discussion group is a warm lead. Anyone who engages with your social media is a cold lead and should be encouraged towards the product for prospects. When you have a warm lead, book a one-on-one meeting with them and present them with your core offer. Some people will buy right away and some will need you to follow up in order to make the sale. Keep a dashboard on the wall where you can see it to track your leads, appointments, presentations and sales.

- **Speed to value:** After someone buys from you, you want to onboard them as a customer and get them started towards their outcome as quickly as possible. You must establish what constitutes value for your clients and see how quickly you can deliver it. Customers pay more for fast, reliable, remarkable results. If your business charges people for time, you will subconsciously want to take longer to deliver value because you will earn more. Over time, this model is destined to fail. If you charge for outcomes, you will be incentivized to figure out the best path to getting your customers what they want – this will result in your business becoming known as being the best.

While doing all of this, keep a close eye on:

- **Cash at bank:** If you run out of cash, it's game over for your business, no matter how promising things are looking. You must set up your business to ensure your cashflow is positive. Bank money in advance of delivering your value – get your customers to pay upfront whenever possible. Squirrel away money into a reserve account for taxes and emergencies. You must never run out of cash.
- **Cost per lead/sale:** Track how much you are spending to win a customer and try to optimize it. You want to discover the allowable cost per sale and then find as many ways as possible for you to spend money and make sales below that amount. Your marketing budgets should actually be marketing ratios. If you understand the portion of every sale you can put back into your marketing, your budget is infinite.
- **Experience scores:** Track and measure a simple question to gauge how well you're looking after your customers: 'How would you rate your experience with us so far out of 10?' Anything less than an 8 is a red flag. Customers

who give you an 8 out of 10 are telling you that they are satisfied but the results they want are coming in a bit too slow. When they start rating you a 6 or a 7, they are telling you that they aren't angry at you but they are disappointed. A 1–5 tells you they are feeling really let down and possibly angry about it. These customers would get a refund or stop paying if possible. Regardless of the score, ask the follow-up question 'Why did you choose that number?' to get actionable feedback.

Activity:

Together with your firestarter team run a planning meeting for the official launch campaign of your business. The launch campaign should engage your ideal customers and create an influx of new paying customers. Your firestarter team should begin the meeting confused about how to launch and leave with clear roles, tasks and outcomes in place.

AI prompt:

'I've been testing a new business and it's shown signs of success. Now it's time to run an official launch campaign. I want to launch in a way that creates a rapid influx of new paying clients. Ask me questions to understand what you need to know about this business and its launch. Then create a step-by-step launch plan and timeline. Also, assist me with all of the marketing content I will need to engage my ideal customers.'

CHAPTER 12

THE CORE TEAM

CORE TEAM PLAYBOOK

MISSION

Maintain a stable lifestyle business that delivers fun, freedom and fulfilment.

TEAM

Key person of influence (you); executive assistant; marketing manager; sales representative; marketing and sales assistant – delivery lead; customer success agent – automation engineer.

OBJECTIVE

Reach a sustainable level of annual revenue covering all costs and greater than 20% net margin. Ensure the whole team are experiencing fun, freedom and fulfilment in their roles.

KEY RESULTS

1. **Perfect repeatable week** campaign brings in greater than 60% of total sales revenue.

2. **Quarterly spotlight** campaigns drive additional profit and create positive engagement with ICPs.

3. Social media accounts have consistent growth and engagement aligned to the **big message**.

4. **Cashflow** is manageable and predictable. Multiple reserve bank accounts for tax, dividends/bonuses and emergencies are in place.

5. **IP, media, data and technology** deliver the majority of value and are instrumental in marketing and sales.

6. Average **customer experience** scores are above 8 out of 10.

7. Financial **forecast and annual plan** is updated and executed smoothly, allowing for holidays, hobbies and passion projects.

8. The business can run with most people working remotely and could easily change jurisdiction if needed.

TECHNIQUES

- Significantly raise the key person of influence status of the founder.
- Founder to prioritize publishing a book, getting on podcasts, increased social media output and public speaking.
- Monday and Friday team meeting and debrief.
- Team discussion groups with active channels (e.g., Slack, WhatsApp).
- Performance dashboard.
- Marketing budget and annual plan based on allowable ratios of spend to results.

- Team pay is base salary plus 20% performance bonuses.
- Team offsite planning session every 90 days.
- Only A-players who exhibit positive attitude and desired skills.

MINDSET

- Dedicated.
- Collaborative.
- Creative.

FAQs

Question	Answer
How to afford first hires?	Hire people on a trial basis and keep them if they can generate a positive return on investment (ROI) within one to three months. Attempt to agree performance-based pay or reduced pay during the trial period. If cash-flow forecasts allow for it, bring good people onto the team as quickly as possible. If possible or necessary, start people on hourly rates or part-time roles. Take pre-sale deposits or upfront payments for clients who will start months in advance. Use that certainty to bring on a team who can support the growth. If someone really special comes along with a commitment for the long haul, be prepared to pay them with equity or profit share. First hires like the executive assistant should generate a ROI based on freeing up the founder's time. A marketing manager or sales role is an ideal performance-based role, especially to begin with.

Question	Answer
How much to pay people?	Check on websites like GlassDoor or Indeed for typical pay scales. Remember that a smaller business offering flexibility, bonuses and mentorship may be able to acquire the right people at the lower end of the scale. Remote foreign workers in places like the Philippines, India or South Africa are often remarkably good value – hard working, skilled, positive and lower pay requirements.
Tech stack budget?	Now is the time to commit to a quality tech stack. You might spend several thousand dollars a month on services like HubSpot, Mailchimp or ActiveCampaign, Slack, Notion, Google Workspace and ScoreApp. You will probably also have a Meta and Google ads account and premium subscriptions to LinkedIn, X.com or Instagram. So long as it saves you or makes you money, it's all part of running a sustainable Lifestyle Business.

'Four sales. Done. E-mail to affiliate partners. Done. New landing page live. Not done. Video testimonials uploaded to YouTube. Done. This week I was really proud that we resolved a client complaint and totally turned them around. I learned that even when we get things wrong, we still have an opportunity to create a positive moment with clients.'

It's Friday afternoon and we always end the week with a quick debrief. We cover the key numbers on our 'Sleep at night dashboard' (SAND) so we can all relax over the weekend. We close out our '3–6 List' with each member of the team – at the beginning of the week, each of us had shared the 3–6 most important things we had planned to do for the week. We end on a high with our biggest learning or magic moments from the week. Then we log off and switch off for the weekend.

It's one of the rituals we have as a core team to make sure we achieve a lot each week, we stay in alignment and we get mental down time.

This team has been in a great rhythm for several years. The business has seven-figure revenue and six-figure profits, even after we all take home a healthy income and performance bonuses. We work together at times in the same office but it's flexible on most days. There's no policing people to see what they are doing hour by hour, we trust that each team member is motivated to achieve their quarterly targets and that's what matters.

This is a team of eight people but our clients think we must have dozens more than that. From the outside we look much bigger than we are. Online we have a strong presence; you can see us regularly uploading content on several social media channels. When we run a quarterly event, hundreds of people show up and it looks like something a huge corporate would take all year to plan and produce. Every week, ads are running, meetings with clients go smoothly, workshops are being delivered, dashboards are updated, e-mail campaigns are delivered and everyone seems to be calm and having fun.

The business is built around my personal brand. I've written a book, I speak on stages, I'm a guest on podcasts and I have a growing social media presence. The team know how to channel all of that attention into LAPS (leads, appointments, presentations and sales). They know how to deliver great value to clients and we regularly get referrals coming in. My role is to be the key person of influence. The team's role is to turn the attention into a sustainable business we all enjoy.

To the degree you can build your personal brand as a key person of influence your business will grow and thrive. Lifestyle businesses really take off when the founder's brand takes off. You must embrace activities like writing a book, speaking on stages, creating videos and podcasts to share your ideas, winning awards and raising your profile on social media. This isn't a narcissistic endeavour – you are building your brand around ideas that add value to others. Your brand will attract the right attention and this will create the opportunity for your team to create a business.

The right people to join your team and build a lifestyle business with you are rebels and misfits. These are people who probably don't naturally fit into a corporate environment. They might be too young or too old for corporate jobs. They might have lots of tattoos, bad acne, a funny accent or a habit of swearing too often. These people know how to roll up their sleeves and get things done. They probably have a background working in hospitality – anyone who's worked in restaurants, nightclubs, cafes, hotels or travel are used to keeping customers happy with razor-thin margins amid an array of nonsense and shenanigans. They probably didn't leave Microsoft to join your team – they've never experienced a free lunch buffet, an IT technician who resets their password or a HR manager who asks them if they want to attend the ukulele playing workshop to help deal with the stress of the air conditioning being broken last Tuesday.

Roles can vary but a typical core team will consist of:

- **Key person of influence:** The public face and strategic visionary of the business. They create content, build the personal brand, attract opportunities and open doors through influence, thought leadership and relationships. Key metric – audience growth and new opportunities in the pipeline.
- **General manager:** The operational leader who turns vision into action. They oversee day-to-day performance, track targets and ensure the business runs smoothly and efficiently. Key metric – the agreed business plan is being delivered and team members hit their key metrics.

- **Head of marketing:** Responsible for driving brand awareness, lead generation and campaign performance. They manage content, advertising, SEO and marketing funnels to ensure a steady stream of qualified leads. Key metrics – marketing qualified leads (MQLs), customer acquisition cost (CAC), conversion rates (CVR), return on ad spend (ROAS).

- **Head of sales and partnerships:** Completes sales and manages high-value relationships. They convert leads into clients, close deals, develop referral partnerships and maximize revenue through scalable sales systems. Key metrics – sales, pipeline value, average deal size, partnership contribution to revenue.

- **Appointment setting:** Focused on supporting sales and marketing to convert leads into sales. They contact leads, qualify interest and book meetings for the sales team to ensure a steady flow of sales conversations. Key metrics – meetings booked, show-up rate, lead-to-meeting conversion rate.

- **Head of tech and media:** Owns the digital infrastructure and media production. They manage websites, software tools, video and audio content, and ensure technology supports business goals and scalability. They upload content to social media and send emails to the database. Key metrics – revenue per employee.

- **Head of customer success:** Ensures clients are on-boarded, supported and thriving. They improve retention, manage support teams and create a remarkable client experience that drives referrals and renewals.

Key metric – experience scores, net promoter score (referrals) and churn or refund rate.

- **Bookkeeping and admin support:** Handles finance and operational admin with precision. They manage invoices, expenses, records and back-office tasks to keep the business compliant, efficient and organized. Key metrics – zero late filings, reconciliation accuracy, admin task completion rate, performance dashboard accuracy.

Not every lifestyle business team will look exactly the same. Some teams might need a few extra salespeople while other teams might require a more complex delivery team. You might have a media person separate from the tech person. The important thing is that your core team doesn't exceed 12 people. When a team is bigger than 12 people it automatically splits into two or three teams. Rather than having one self-organizing coherent team you will have a sales team who don't talk to the operations team. Your reaction to this divide will be to put in place systems and procedures that kill the flat, autonomous culture that gives you an edge. Above 12 people on a core team you will find you are too big to be small and too small to be big.

This doesn't mean you can't have suppliers. A supplier is not part of the core team. If your business finds a great graphic designer who produces work to a high standard on your budget, that person is an excellent resource the whole team can leverage but they're not part of the core team. The core team are the people who sign on to take part in the key rituals of being on the team.

The core team rituals are a set of consistent, high-leverage practices that keep the team aligned, focused and energized. These rituals create rhythm, transparency and accountability across the business. These are my top six rituals for a core team:

- **Monday morning meeting:** A weekly 30-minute sync to set the tone for the week. Each leader shares their top 3–6 priorities and any support they need. The team moves forward with clarity and momentum for the week ahead. Note: During times of rapid growth or change, this could go back to being a daily huddle.

- **Friday afternoon debrief:** A 30-minute, reflective session to celebrate wins, capture lessons and flag issues. Each team member closes the loop on their 3–6 priorities for the week by sharing their list and saying 'done' or 'not done'. They then share a magic moment from the week or something they learned. It closes the week with accountability, insights and gratitude.

- **Quarterly retreat:** A strategic offsite to step back from the day-to-day, review performance, reset goals and reconnect as a team. This is typically a lunch and half-day meeting in a boardroom. The focus is planning out the next 90 days, dealing with any of the bigger issues and brainstorming big ideas. It's where alignment and inspiration are renewed.

- **Core comms channel:** The central, real-time communication hub (e.g., Slack, Teams or WhatsApp) where all updates, questions and check-ins happen in real time.

It's designed to replace unnecessary meetings and scattered messages. It's designed so the whole team can be up to date on everything even if they are working remotely or on flexible hours.

- **Central database and storage:** The single source of truth for company documents, brand assets, media content and client data. Organized, searchable and accessible to the team at all times it should never be hard to find the right document, export some data or find a video file to upload to social media.

- **Sleep at night dashboard:** A live dashboard that tracks the most important metrics – revenue, leads, customer satisfaction and system health might be the main metrics – so everyone can instantly know how the business is performing at a glance. Any metric that would give you peace of mind, or sound the alarm if something was wrong should be updated regularly to this dashboard. The basic goal is to be able to see this dashboard on Friday and then completely switch off from business for the weekend.

Your core team is in place, you are following your rituals so now it's time to ensure you are focused on the main activities that really drive performance. The most important activities are:

- **Perfect repeatable week:** Great businesses don't make it up from scratch each week, they repeat what works. Set your targets for the year and then break them down into 40–45 perfect repeatable weeks. Craft your ideal rhythm of high-impact activities that move the business forward and consistently execute the same things every week. It includes running your standard marketing campaigns, delivering sales meetings and responding to customer service queries. The more you formalize the bulk of what you do into a perfect repeatable week template, the more it frees up mental space for creativity.

- **Quarterly spotlight:** Each quarter, the business focuses its attention on one clear campaign, offer or initiative. This spotlight aligns marketing, sales and customer success around a novel message and creates momentum by doing something new or different. You might have a quarterly event you host or you could sponsor existing events that you feature prominently at. You might have a quarterly spotlight campaign focused on a special offer, limited edition product or seasonal campaign. A spotlight campaign is a great way to re-engage people who responded to your weekly marketing campaigns but didn't buy anything and forgot about you. The key is to make it exciting and engaging but to stay at a level that your small team can manage.

- **Annual big message:** A flagship idea that defines the year. It's the narrative that shapes keynote talks, major content pieces, PR outreach and thought leadership from the key person of influence. The big message comes to life on podcasts, social media channels, blogs or even a book you publish. It's not about the product or service you offer, it is about sharing a bigger more philosophical stance. It gives your brand coherence and authority in the market.

- **Customer delight:** Beyond delivering what was promised, your team plan and deliver moments of surprise, recognition and genuine care. A delighted customer becomes a loyal advocate driving the word-of-mouth referrals that make your business highly profitable. It's useful to imagine that your business is a manufacturer of delighted customers. When they think about the money they spent with you, they would enthusiastically spend it again. This happens when they get what they expect and then some.

- **IP capture:** As you solve problems, build systems, deliver value and create happy customers you're also generating intellectual property (IP). Capturing this in frameworks, templates, scripts, videos, books and case studies builds a moat around the business and makes it more scalable. Unless you pause, reflect and document your IP, this valuable asset will be lost. Reinforce the value of IP in your whole team so they can spot it, capture it, develop it and protect it.

- **Asset creation:** Every quarter should leave behind valuable, new assets. An asset is anything that would continue to deliver value even if all of your team disappeared. Like physical assets, digital assets are built to last and are typically created when you collaborate with a high-quality supplier who uses your IP to produce something outstanding such as media, websites, code, workbooks, software, books, podcast episodes and the like. Once developed, digital assets can be reused, repurposed or monetized at speed and scale.

- **Product ecosystem:** The fully developed product and service ecosystem creates the profit for the business. You can't build a great business on just one product or service. Your team need to build out four categories – gifts, products for prospects, core offer and products for clients. Your business needs high-quality gifts that you can give away to attract attention. It needs products for prospects to get people to engage. You need a valuable core offering (in a few variations) to deliver a remarkable transformation to your customers. You will need products for clients so after people buy the core offering they can continue the journey and maintain new standards. These products will link smoothly together so people can effortlessly test you out, gain trust and then become a paying customer who buys many times from you and refers their friends.

A strong core team, with valuable rituals, focused on powerful activities is the key to a lasting lifestyle business. This is where your life changes dramatically. Getting paid to travel around the world will become normal. Starting your day when you feel ready and finishing when you feel done will become common. Working three or four days a week will become a viable choice. You'll earn more than a big business could pay you – all of that money they spend on offices, managers, brand building, HR and pointless meetings will go straight to your bottom line. You'll be able to pick and choose your direction, your clients and your pace of life. Business will become a way of living not a way of eking out a living.

Activity:

Create a picture of what your lifestyle business will be like when it reaches the end state of a core team that is stable, profitable and fun. Then create a financial forecast of what your business will look like when it gets to this level. Imagine how many customers you will have, what they will be buying, how much they will spend on average and what your total sales revenue will be. Then imagine all of the costs you will have for running this business including the team, marketing and advertising, costs to deliver value and general expenses. Create a future-state snapshot of the perfect lifestyle boutique you will own in the future.

Use BookMagic.ai to write a thought leadership book that positions you as a key person of influence.

Use AwardsApp.ai to enter and win an award that positions your business at the top of its category.

AI prompt:

'I want to create a highly profitable lifestyle business with 6–12 core team members. I want this business to be stable, sustainable, profitable and fun. Ask me questions to better understand the business I want to create and then create a future forecast of what it will look like when it is in an ideal state. Forecast the revenue streams, as well as the costs and the profitability. Give me the job roles my team will consist of and the marketing and business activities that will most likely keep the business functioning as a stable and successful lifestyle business.'

DO NOT READ THE NEXT CHAPTER

You're good! You have the lifestyle business.

You have a team of 6–12 people. You have rituals and activities that keep you profitable and having fun. You are earning in the top 5% of people in the developed world. Your life is running tax efficiently. You can do most things you want to do whenever you want to do them. Life is good. What more do you want?

You're about to make a critical error – you think more will be better. You think going bigger would give you more out of life. You justify it in many ways – bigger impact, more profit, less dependence on you and a life-changing exit are just a few bold moves away. Maybe you don't even think about it; maybe you just let things grow naturally.

It's a trap. There is a very high chance that you are getting the most rewards for the least effort from your business and you are going to make your life harder for marginal gains by growing beyond this point. What you should be doing is diversifying your interests. You should be leaning into community work, spending time with friends and family, investing your money into a portfolio of assets, getting fitter and healthier than ever, writing a book while taking a month off, having a kid, restoring a classic car, hosting a charity ball or learning to DJ. Do anything but grow your business beyond 12 people on the core team.

When you grow a team of people beyond 12, the team will divide into two or three units. You will probably have a sales team, an ops team, an admin team and a leadership team. You used to have two quick meetings per week to get the whole team into flow, now you're having a dozen meetings a week and you haven't even seen any customers yet. You need more experienced managers. You need a marketing manager, a sales manager and an operations manager who know how to do things at the next level. You hire them and they immediately tell you that for them to do their job they each need to make a few more hires, subscribe to some fancy software tools and start using some bigger agencies. You go with their suggestions and now you have eye-watering overheads.

Your team swells up to 18 people pretty quickly. Two people on your team start dating. Another two have a massive falling out. Wastage is rife – everywhere you look you discover money being spent with no return. One day you've got your head down in a proposal document evaluating an expensive recommendation from a fancy agency and there's a phone call from one of your top people. They are calling to hand in their notice – you've not spoken to them in months, it turns out they really preferred the way the company used to run and they are leaving to do their next thing.

You arrive back from speaking at a conference, you're exhausted because you were working on the plane and didn't get much sleep. These trips used to generate pure profit but now you feel like you have to do them just to keep the lights on. When you walk into the office (because you have an office now) you're met with one of the newer members of your team. She wants to talk about some grievances she has with her manager. Stupidly, you treat the meeting too casually and say something fairly harmless like 'maybe this role isn't right for you?' You didn't mean it in a nasty way, in your mind you were exploring proactive options to resolve the issue. A week later you get a legal letter and you are being sued for constructive dismissal; your lawyer tells you to just settle it for six months' severance pay and move on. You can't believe this business has gone from being a dream to being a nightmare so quickly.

If you are going to grow your team beyond 12 people, you need to commit to going all the way up over 30 people. Only when you get to 30+ people will things become enjoyable again, but it won't be like the good old days of your lifestyle business. When you get to 30 people, you'll be a new type of business – a performance business.

To get to a lifestyle business, you need to be focused about 80% on what your business does for customers and 20% on the way you run the business. This ratio will reverse as you get bigger and become a performance business. You will have to become a business geek who reads books on business strategy, watched videos about cultivating organizational culture, listens to podcasts on nuanced pricing strategies and attends workshops about financial management.

The performance business will be more grown up. You'll have detailed dashboards, software and spreadsheets. Your team will consist of people who are more professional in their approach. You'll probably have debt or investors. You'll see your customers a lot less. You might start to feel like the business is not so much an extension of you, but it has a life of its own and sometimes you'll feel like you aren't a good fit for its culture. Your leadership team will run a tight ship and will tell you what they want you to do – sometimes it will seem like you're a dancing monkey who bangs the symbols on command. People will get hired and decisions will get made that you have nothing to do with. Your margins will halve but profit and your valuation will grow and grow. The business might start spitting off serious dividends or sell for an eye-popping sum of money.

Is it worth it? Maybe. Let's be real – if it were easy to create a valuable business then everyone would do it and if everyone could do it, it wouldn't be valuable. The only reason businesses sell for millions is because they are really hard to create. Big companies already know it's cheaper and easier to buy a business that exists than it is to create one from scratch. The chances of building a business with a huge profit or valuation are very slim but the stress and aggravation that comes with trying to do it is guaranteed.

For most entrepreneurs, especially if you liked the title of this book, the juice is not worth the squeeze. You are better off keeping your lifestyle business as a boutique operation that is full of fun, freedom, flexibility and fulfilment.

With that said, if you want to take a peak at what the next level up looks like, then read on – but be careful what you wish for.

CHAPTER 13

THE PERFORMANCE TEAM

PERFORMANCE TEAM PLAYBOOK (OPTIONAL)

MISSION

Double enterprise value every two years until you are able to sell the business for a life-changing amount of money.

LEADERSHIP TEAM

Founder/chief executive officer (CEO), chief operating officer (COO), chief marketing officer (CMO), chief technology officer (CTO), chief information officer (CIO)/chief financial officer (CFO), executive assistant.

BOARD

Founder/CEO plus four board members.

OPERATIONAL TEAMS

Preferred: Growth, delivery, data and insights.

Alternatively: Teams focused on products, territories or markets.

OBJECTIVE

Build towards an exit by establishing predictable revenue (preferably contracted), proprietary assets and an exceptional team.

Alternatively: Continue top line growth or maximize profitability.

KEY RESULTS

1. Annualized recurring **revenue growth of 20%+.**
2. **EBITDA 20%+** with no abnormal accounting issues.
3. **Employee retention indicators above 8 out of 10.**
4. Founder works less than 30 hours/week (tracked) and mostly in a **figurehead role.**
5. Intangible assets like database size, media library, intellectual property, systems, brand and culture are clearly documented in a **virtual data room.**
6. Financial forecasts, business plans and regulatory compliance is **up to date.**
7. Business advisor or broker relationship established with **intention to sell.**

TECHNIQUES

- Quarterly leadership and team retreats.
- Recruit next-level talent.
- Investment into special long-term business assets.
- Award bonuses on recurring revenue through contracts, memberships or subscriptions.
- Research industry benchmarks.

- Scrutinize and cut non-performing expenses, clean up financial mess or confusion and conduct external assessments and reports.
- Identify 30+ potential acquirers such as private equity funds, strategic acquirers or an employee ownership scheme.
- Create a detailed 2–3 year plan to exit.
- Conduct annual business assessment and valuation from an external advisor.

MINDSET

- Accountable.
- Systematic.
- Strategic.

FAQs

Question	Answer
Is it worth selling a business?	Normally you won't want to sell a business that can be sold. By the time it is saleable, it will be a prized possession for you. You may wish to sell it to retire, to diversify wealth or because you enjoy starting something new. Even a large sale may not improve your life as much as you imagine because the business that warrants a high price is typically wildly profitable, with a great culture and a bright future.

Question	Answer
Who should be on the board?	The founder and maybe one other person from the leadership team, someone from a bigger business, someone who scrutinizes the numbers, someone who understands the market you sell to and someone who has been part of a business sale (or several). These people can be paid a quarterly fee to attend meetings and may also get a bonus upon a successful exit.
How to keep the team motivated while I'm focused on a sale?	Explore a profit-share pool (e.g., 10% of EBITDA allocated quarterly), empower new leaders in the company, ensure high-impact quarterly retreats. Enter respected awards and grant bonuses for being a finalist or winner.

'Last month, one of the business units did over $1 million in new sales which was a new high, you should drop them an e-mail. Profit for that team is now forecasting at more than $250,000 per month.

We need to pay the lawyers another $75,000 for the work they did on the completed acquisition, are you happy to sign off on it today?

Subscription revenue is stalling at $750,000 per month for the core SaaS offering. Our churn rate is far too high; we want to bring in a few churn specialists to sort it out, can you ask around for a recommendation?

We've been offered a $900,000 loan if we want it, the interest rate is 11% and we can decide if we want it in the next 30 days.

The new marketing campaign has an acceptable CAC, and based on the ROAS we're going to scale up ads to $100,000 per month.

There's another PE firm who wants to talk shop about a potential deal – do you want to do the meeting or should we send in the CFO to suss them out first? Also, the dashboard is showing a few red flags for net promoter scores (NPS) on our new AI-portal. I'm getting that great little agency in Toronto to take a closer look.

We won a gold award for customer service last week, can you make a video for social media?

There's a company in Australia contesting our IP registration in that territory, it'll be about $45,000 to fight it out with them or we can enter into a settlement agreement that restricts the way we can use our logo in that region – which way are you leaning?'

All of this excitement isn't that exciting anymore. This is a typical meeting with my assistant and one of my leadership team running through the issues of the week. There was a time when any of these updates – legal threats, record sales, awards, big expenses – would be either a cause for a champagne-popping celebration or a mental melt-down. Neither the good stuff or the bad stuff phases me anymore, it's all just stuff. I'm a business geek now and I've seen all of this before in one form or another.

A business hits the performance zone at about 30 people. It becomes a different type of business to the lifestyle business it was a few years earlier. Back in the good old days, you recruited people who seemed fun and enthusiastic and you offered them a job on the spot. Now you recruit carefully from a pool of carefully selected candidates provided to you from a specialist recruiter. Your culture used to be felt by the team, now it's codified in the on-boarding document. Your most important number that you tracked was the cash balance in the bank, now you have detailed spreadsheets and management reports explaining exactly which levers to pull and how hard.

You still love your business but it's a different type of love. Your smaller lifestyle business really felt like an extension of you and your performance business feels like it's got a life of its own. Your lifestyle boutique felt a bit silly, playful and irreverent. It sometimes felt like it would die at any moment if you weren't keeping it alive. Your performance business feels like it doesn't need you as much for its survival. It's a bit more serious, more strategic and robust in its design now.

You have a decision to make.

Will you evolve to become the leader of a bigger more professional team?

Will you stay the eccentric rebel-founder, half-genius and half liability?

Will you sell the business to some grownups and go find your next adventure?

Before you decide, let's take a look at the components of your performance business – the leadership team:

- **CEO – chief executive officer** (normally this is still the founder): The visionary and difficult decision-maker. Owns the strategy, shapes the narrative and steers the leadership team toward a mission and vision. The CEO cultivates key relationships, congratulates performers, speaks on behalf of the company, disrupts people's thinking, spots important trends, smooths out disputes, finds resources and reminds people what's really important.
- **COO – chief operating officer:** The executor. Turns strategy into systems, ensuring operations hum, departments are aligned and targets are hit. This is the person who's running the business day to day, having one-to-ones with the team, holding suppliers accountable, surfacing and solving issues and making sure the CEO doesn't break too many things all at once.
- **CMO – chief marketing officer:** The growth architect. Designs and drives campaigns that build the brand, generate leads and convert attention into action. Tracks marketing metrics like CAC, ROAS, LTV and pipeline velocity with ruthless precision. Finds whip-smart suppliers to growth hack the latest marketing tactics into reality, talks to the sales team and customer success to find out what's happening downstream and how it can shape the broader marketing message.

- **CTO – chief technology officer:** The automation brain. Ensures the tech stack is scalable, secure and aligned to customer needs. They manage engineers, developers and software integrations while obsessing over features and reliability. They research tech trends, they fear being late to implement a leapfrog technology but they also know it can be dangerous to chase every shiny gadget that comes along. They want technology to eliminate drudgery and free up humans to do more human stuff.

- **CIO or CFO – chief information officer or chief financial officer:** The number cruncher. The business spits out a lot of data. Some of it is financial and some of it is performance related. This person is across all of it. They have detailed financial forecasts and can predict what will happen if you choose to zig or zag. They rarely come up with big new ideas but they are excellent at mapping out big ideas into logical models and telling you if your ideas are worth pursuing. They also keep the business compliant with the tax office, shareholders up to date and lenders in good standing.

- **EA – executive assistant:** The glue that holds the leadership team together to maximize executive focus. They handle scheduling, correspondence, follow-ups and admin with precision, acting as a gatekeeper, amplifier and trusted confidante. A high-level EA doesn't just support, they anticipate. They protect the attention of the leadership team and ensure important things get done without noise or drama. Armed with AI, this person is a high-agency generalist who is able to do a little bit of everything.

ALIGNING YOUR TEAMS AND BUILDING CULTURE

Your leadership team must get into alignment around your vision for the future and the missions that need to be achieved. Only when they are functioning as a tight unit can you expect the whole business to unleash its potential. Taking the team away on leadership retreats is an essential feature of performance. During a retreat, you want to face up to harsh realities, have tough discussions, formulate plans that are best for the business and get total buy-in from all of the leaders.

When you leave the retreat, everyone will know what is expected of them and their team in the months ahead. Each leader will go out and get their divisional teams aligned around the most important initiatives. Leaders will be excited to unlock bonuses for themselves and their teams when they hit clear goals. They will dread the thought of turning up to the next leadership retreat and reporting their subpar performance.

Each leader will have a divisional team that they run and improve constantly. Their divisional teams will run like core teams with live dashboards, regular huddles and clear communication. Every individual will understand the bigger picture of what the company is trying to achieve and they will know what their role is in achieving the broader mission.

Your company needs to be highly intentional about the culture you want to build. Culture can be measured by behaviour under pressure. Many companies say the right things on their website about innovation, communication, boldness or collaboration. The true test is not what they say, it's what they do and what gets rewarded or punished. Some people want to be part of a fast-paced, high-intensity culture that demands focus and commitment at the cost of comfort or flexibility.

Some people want to be part of a culture that is more gentle, calm, flexible and balanced with other areas of life. One culture isn't better than another, the problem is when people expect one thing and get another.

It's OK for the Royal Marines to be demanding on their recruits because people know what they are getting themselves into. It's not OK to tell people that your business is all about fun, freedom and fulfilment and then demand that they do stressful jobs, with endless deadlines and no rewards.

Your leadership team needs to be clear about the behaviours that will be expected and rewarded so they can cultivate a divisional team who understand and want what's on offer.

DIVISIONAL TEAMS

With your leadership team in place, the business naturally extends into divisional teams that deliver the actual results. These teams may be structured around functions, regions or customer segments, depending on the business model. In most performance businesses, there are three core divisions that form the operational backbone:

- **Growth team:** This is the revenue engine of the business. This team drives awareness, attracts leads and converts them into paying customers.

  - **Marketing:** Owns the brand, message and attention strategy. They craft campaigns, generate leads and optimize every step of the marketing journey.

From paid media to e-mail nurture sequences, search engine optimization (SEO), social media, joint ventures and sponsorships, they work to fill the pipeline with high-quality prospects.

○ **Sales:** Converts interest into income. They set appointments, hold discovery calls, follow up, close deals, build relationships, collect referrals and develop partnerships. A high-performing sales team is disciplined, metrics-driven and aligned to marketing for seamless lead flow. This team ensures that what was sold gets delivered. This team is building out the products and services and making sure customers get the value they signed up for.

- **Delivery team:**

  ○ **Product development:** Owns the customer experience and value delivery. Whether it's a digital product, SaaS platform, coaching programme, done-for-you service, consulting or course, this team is always improving, iterating and staying ahead of expectations. This team turn ideas into formalized intellectual property, code, content and frameworks that customers experience when they buy. They are seeking the most efficient and scalable way of leaving customers delighted, time and time again.

  ○ **Customer success:** Keeps clients happy, supported and coming back for more. They manage on-boarding, support, renewals and upgrades. They measure themselves based on retention, net promoter score (NPS), lifetime value (LTV) and five-star reviews. They are the human side of a scalable offer. The silent power behind the scenes. This team keeps everything organized, measured and moving. Without them, chaos creeps in.

- **Insights and admin team:**

  ○ **Data and insights:** Translates numbers into knowledge. They build dashboards, track metrics, analyze performance and generate the insights that guide strategy and execution. They keep track of the financial data and the performance data of the business and they can link them up to find hidden bottlenecks or growth levers. They help leaders make better decisions, faster.

  ○ **Admin and operations support:** Ensures the business is buttoned-up and compliant. From invoicing and contracts to scheduling and HR processes, they make sure the gears turn without grinding. Their job is invisible until it's not — and that's the sign of excellence.

Each of these teams plays a critical role in your performance business – not just in doing work, but in scaling value. In a high-functioning company, these aren't just departments – they are **integrated systems** with clear outcomes, aligned incentives and measurable contribution to growth.

THREE BUSINESS PLANS

There are essentially three business plans your performance business can adopt. Of course you will do a bit of all three but it's powerful to pick a dominant focus at any given time.

GROW THE REVENUE

This is the plan to increase top-line income. This is the most visible and exciting plan for your team and it's typically the plan most entrepreneurs and founders naturally gravitate to. It focuses on lead generation, sales conversions, pricing strategy and customer acquisition. Tactics include new campaigns, product launches, market expansion and channel partnerships. Growth, even when it's not profitable, feels exciting. To make it sustainable you have to have a way of funding the growth and a plan to make it profitable eventually. If you discover that your business offers something fresh and unique and it has a high gross margin, it can be very wise to go all-in on scaling-up as big and fast as you can, even if it means your profit margins suffer through the expansion.

Key metrics: new sales, monthly recurring revenue (MRR), annual recurring revenue (ARR), average deal size, pipeline velocity.

GROW THE PROFITABILITY

This is the plan to improve margins and drive more profit from existing revenue to bottom line. It includes optimizing costs, increasing efficiency, raising prices, reducing churn and leveraging automation. This plan requires adopting more granular reporting, tightening up on standards, being intolerant of waste, stripping out unnecessary processes and reducing the number of people required to deliver the same outcome. This plan is more scary and demotivating for most teams – you want this to be a plan you execute quickly while you also manage expectations and energy in the team with all the leadership skill you can muster. In the short term, it's not fun making cuts to spending but in the aftermath the business is remarkably improved. You free up money for growth, you reduce the burden of poor performance and the business becomes more valuable.

Key metrics: net profit, gross margin, cost of delivery, CAC-to-LTV ratio, earnings before interest, taxes, depreciation and amortization (EBITDA).

GROW THE VALUATION AND EXIT THE BUSINESS

This is the plan to build an investable or saleable asset. You are preparing for a partial exit, private equity transaction, strategic merger or full sale. This plan has your team focused on formalizing and documenting your unique intellectual property, systems and processes. You'll be cleaning up accounts, strengthening recurring revenue, reducing founder-dependency and identifying strategic acquirers or investors. It's about making the business more valuable than its basic numbers first suggest – you are working on improving 'the multiple' you will be valued on when you present your numbers. You will create a virtual data-room that makes it easy for an investor or acquirer to see your financial data, performance data, assets, forecasts and documentation. You will have a clear plan and financial forecast as to how your business can double and then double again. You will identify a list of strategic acquirers who would benefit in many ways from the purchase of your business and would not want their competitors to get hold of your main assets. All of these steps make your business more valuable and enhance the chances of a transaction taking place.

Key metrics: valuation multiples, recurring revenue percentage of total revenue, founder dependency, strategic moat, proprietary assets, acquisition interest.

In the context of a lifestyle business, the more your business becomes a performance business, the less it will inherently be linked to your lifestyle. In the early days, you and your business were one – a performance business is its own entity. You can of course build your performance business to fuel your lifestyle choices. Growth can be a lot of fun and take you to amazing places, literally and emotionally. Profitability can deliver you the cash you want to have adventures or transform treasured causes you hold dear. The sale of your business is a life-changing event that will morph you from being an entrepreneur into being a wealth manager almost overnight. You'll need to learn a whole new set of skills and will discover the entrepreneurial mindset can get you in a lot of trouble when you are supposed to be a sober custodian of your money.

Quite ironically, as your performance business grows, you will likely reminisce about the good old days when the team was small and the day-to-day was fun and adventurous. You may harbour a secret desire to start something new and deliberately keep it as a boutique. It's entirely possible you will do what many 'post-exit' entrepreneurs have done and write a book, speak on stages, create some new intellectual property, craft an offer and hire a small team of 6–12 people. You will have had a visceral experience of performance businesses and might deliberately choose to stay at the point where you get the maximum enjoyment – you'll create your perfect lifestyle business.

Activity:

Work with an experienced finance professional to create a detailed financial forecast and business plan to transform your business into a performance business. This plan should show you month-by-month income and expenditure for the next five years. The plan should seem logical and achievable. Explore ways of transforming your business so that you maximize recurring revenue, technology development, growth and profitability. Discuss ways to move your business towards a higher exit multiple and construct a valuation estimate for the business you will create five years from now.

AI prompt:

'I want to transform my small business into a bigger, more valuable business that could be sold in a strategic acquisition or a private equity transaction. Ask me questions to determine the strengths and weaknesses of my current business and then construct a plan for me to transform it into a more valuable business that could be sold for a life-changing amount of money. Give me the vision, mission and values of my future business. Show me the organization chart and role descriptions for when the business has at least 30 employees. Give me a day-of-exit profit and loss forecast. Give me a list of potential acquirers and the strategic reason they would invest in my business.'

CHAPTER 14

NOW IS THE MOMENT TO CREATE YOUR LIFESTYLE BUSINESS

Every so often the world fundamentally changes. Something happens that upends the system as we know it and a completely new way of living dawns. This doesn't happen in most people's lifetimes. Most people who have ever lived were born and died in a system that didn't change much during their lifetime. They were born into a tribe and died in a tribe. They were born into a farming family and died in a farming family. They were born in a factory town and died in a factory town. Most people in history did what their parents did. Most people who have ever lived didn't witness a massive change to where they could live or how they could live.

Your life is different. You are alive at a time of radical change. Regardless of what your parents did for work or where you grew up, the world is your oyster. You can design your life the way you want it to a degree most of civilization wouldn't dare thinking about. The world around you is changing and you get to decide how you will respond to it.

Imagine being a farmer during the time tractors were invented. Imagine being a fine tailor when sewing machines came out. Imaging being a housewife when white goods were rolled out. Imagine being a horse trainer when cars were making their way onto the roads.

These technologies were both liberating and disruptive. They required a response. Your life simply couldn't go on as normal. You would have had to rethink your entire way of life or sit around doing nothing all day.

Society radically changes when general-purpose technologies are rolled out. These are technologies that can be used in hundreds of new ways to achieve countless breakthroughs. The printing press, steam and petrol engines, electricity, plastics and factory production lines are all examples of general-purpose technologies that changed the world.

These types of breakthroughs used to happen every few thousand years. The transitions from the Stone Age to Bronze Age and Iron Age are measured in centuries and millennia.

In the last few decades, however, general-purpose technologies have been rolling out general-purpose technologies every few years. Personal computers, the internet, GPS, social media, smartphones and now generative AI are all recent examples of technology that cause a wholesale change in society. If you are old enough to remember back to before 2000, you know life then was different and most of the changes spring from digital technologies being widely adopted.

AI isn't just another general-purpose technology, it's a technology that disrupts our entire economic system globally. AI already does a lot of the work some of the smartest, most diligent humans who have ever lived struggle to do. AI is doing the heavy lifting in investment banking, law, medicine, engineering, scientific research, design and coding. Anything it isn't currently able to do, it's rapidly catching up. AI agents are already turning simple commands into a set of tasks it can complete in the real world. The most complex work is becoming simplified and carried out by AI to an extent that a novice can do things only a genius could do not long ago.

AI is plugging into devices. AI will power robots, drones and vehicles. All sorts of things in the physical world are becoming automated or massively simplified. AI is plugging into quantum computing and will discover the underlying order of the universe at a level humans couldn't comprehend. AI isn't limited by geographical borders, human lifespans or our typical speeds of communication or thought. We've created something so powerful we do not know where it will take us.

What we do know is that work as we know it is going away. As it stands, any income that enters your household comes from one of four places:

- Allocated benefits assigned to you from government.
- Wages derived from selling your time and skills at a fixed rate.

- Performance income derived from achieving outcomes (e.g., commissions, bonuses, profit from a business you run).
- Asset income derived from what you own (e.g., royalties, rent, interest, dividends from businesses you don't run).

Wages are going away. Not necessarily for everyone and not all at once but technology will remove a lot of wages from the system. As we venture beyond 2030, robots and AI will do most things better, cheaper, faster and safer than humans can. As humans are removed from more and more traditional jobs, the jobs that remain will be more and more competitive. There will be a collapse in the value of standardized time for money.

Wages as we know them today are a relatively recent phenomenon. For most of civilization, people were paid for tasks as they were completed not at regular intervals in a fixed amount. The fixed income model of wages arose out of the industrialized factory. Workers were seen as standardized parts in a process of production and it made sense to pay them a standardized wage. This is going to become increasingly rare as anything standardized in nature will be replaced by technology.

What remains for humans to do will be outcome based. Humans will sell products, services, experiences and access to community on a unit-by-unit basis. Humans will do the messy stuff. The important stuff for humans to do is the stuff requiring you to be part visionary, entertainer, researcher, physical labourer, psychologists, marketer and organizing force. The ability to context switch, to feel emotions one minute and think clearly the next, to carry a box and then enter a thoughtful prompt is going to be uniquely human. This is exactly what it's like being part of a small entrepreneurial team.

The hallmark of the industrialized system was standardized components organized centrally. The hallmark of the Digital Age is unique, fluid, energizing and decentralized. The Industrial Age wanted humans to be part of the machine. The Digital Age wants humans to be creators. This sounds wonderful but it comes with a big condition – creators need to perform. The Industrial Age rewarded workers for turning up and doing basic, repeatable tasks. The Digital Age only rewards people for performance outcomes and most people aren't ready for it.

Unless you want to be dependent on the government, you must get good at delivering outcomes or you must own assets that can't be taken from you by governments that are trying to fund massive welfare programmes. The government will have to pay for millions of people who aren't prepared for the post-AI world of work. To do this they will print money and in doing so they will inflate the value of real assets like houses, shares and precious metals. At a certain point enormous sums of the wealth will be stored in these assets and the governments will want that money back – they will implement small wealth taxes and then ramp them up year after year. They will partner with massive fund managers to buy back the assets from people who can't afford the taxes. They will make it very hard to own anything of value and they will expect you to be happy about it.

There is an exception to this rule. We are a long way from governments being able to recognize digital assets as actual assets they can tax into oblivion. The government won't see your social media profiles as assets in their own right. They won't understand that content is an asset and code is an asset. They won't see the bond and connection you have with people all over the world as an asset. They won't put a value on intellectual property that isn't formalized in a traditional way. These decentralized assets are powerful because they help you to achieve outcomes.

The post-AI world will reward you for outcomes you can achieve at speed. Any asset that gives you a permanent advantage in achieving fast outcomes is an asset that allows you to be free. Your database, your brand, creative process, frameworks, content and code are all examples of these assets. These assets travel with you wherever you go. So long as you and your team have your phones and an internet connection, you can achieve outcomes at speed and earn money from anywhere in the world. This will be no small thing – you will have fun, freedom, flexibility and fulfilment.

AI and other technologies are going to disrupt everything and everyone. We can't see around this corner but it's obvious that millions of new products and services will be created. New business models will be made possible. Small dynamic teams can explore these changes and many millions of people will make great fortunes in doing so.

The Industrial Age had a plan for your life. You would go to school for about 15 years, then you would be a worker for 30 years. You'd then join the ranks of management for

10 years and then become a leader for 5 years. After that, you would retire for 15 years and then die. Along the way you would be able to buy a house and have it paid off just in time for retirement. When you died, the sale of your house would cover outstanding taxes or bills you had and any remaining money would help your children to continue on the same path.

The Digital Age doesn't adhere to this way of living and working – it wants you to complete loops of performance. In the Digital Age, you discover a problem, research it, assemble a team, devise a solution, scale the solution, then hand it over or close it down. Your ability to earn is linked to your ability to execute this formula over and over again. These loops are highly valuable in the digital economy. Completing some of these loops can earn you more money in a few years than most people earn in their entire life. If you notice a big problem, assemble a wickedly smart team, build and scale a robust solution and then hand it over to an acquirer in a lucrative deal – you may never need to do anything else economically.

The idea of a lifestyle business is attractive. At a surface level, it conjures up a vision of travelling the world, visiting beach bars, golfing, shopping and laughing out loud with your friends about how you never need to worry or work again. What if this lifestyle wasn't enough though? What if I told you achieving this vision of a lifestyle business wouldn't feel fulfilling for more than a few months?

There is nothing more exhilarating than completing creative loops with the right people. This isn't work, this is what the human spirit is designed for. Being part of a small group of creative people solving meaningful problems at scale feels incredible. It feels better than sitting on a beach, lazing around a big home or endlessly consuming resources. The reason most entrepreneurs keep going even after they've made a lot of money is because they adore the game. They crave the feeling of being part of a team, struggling together to solve a thrilling problem. Nothing beats it.

In this fast-changing world, your environment will dictate your performance. The people and places you spend time around will transform the quality of your life. If you choose to spend time with people who are terrified by change, you will be dragged down into their helplessness. If you spend time with entrepreneurs and visionaries who see opportunity and prosperity it will rub off on you too.

The most important choice you can make today is to enrol yourself into groups of people who are creating and building with hope and optimism. You want to be around people who share best practices they discover, who collaborate, hold each other accountable to high standards and connect you up with resources you need. These people and places are out there already. Being part of these communities is what makes me so confident that the future will be bright. It's true that many things will have to break before they can be rebuilt even better. A lot of inevitable change is coming down the pipelines. It's people like you who will have the ability to steer the world from a place of love and creativity.

Do not be afraid. You are from a long line of survivors. You have two parents, four grandparents, eight great-grandparents and sixteen great-great-grandparents.

They all lived through radical changes too. All told, you have over a million direct ancestors who lived in the last 500 years. For you to be here, they survived through illness, extreme weather, wars, famine and plague. They all had to meet someone, share a first kiss and start a family. For you to be here, all of them had to survive and make babies.

Every single one of them would look at your life right now and be in awe. Every one of them would trade places with you in a heartbeat. All of them would marvel at the opportunity that lays before you. You owe it to them to make the most of this moment. To seize the day and harness the opportunity that has arrived. For the first time in your family tree, the world is truly your oyster. You can travel, learn, create and share at warp-speed. You can solve exciting problems at scale.

You may think you want to be free from problems. What you really want is meaningful problems and the right people around you excitedly creating solutions to them. It will shock you how vapid it feels to have no problems and how wonderful it feels to find a problem you're drawn to. Ironically your lifestyle business will happen when you aren't focused on your lifestyle. You'll be focusing on improving the lives of others.

Be brave. Have fun. Make a dent in the universe.

ACKNOWLEDGMENTS

Business is a team sport. None of my successes are my own and none of my shortcomings could have been overcome without others. My 'lifestyle' is only possible because of the people I have around me.

To my wife Aléna, thank you for your support, wisdom and partnership.

Thank you to my business partners and friends Glen Carlson, Steven Oddy, Mike Reid, Lucy McCarraher, Joe Gregory, Johnathan Farrah, Donna O'Toole, Topher Morrison, Martin Huntbach, Lyndsay Cambridge. Thanks to my amazing assistant Suzy Mudd and CFO David Horne.

My mentors Jeremy Harbour, Alexis Sikorsky. Thanks to Steven Bartlett, Ali Abdaal and Chris Do for making me a bit famous.

Thanks to the entire teams at Dent, ScoreApp, BookMagic, AwardsApp, August Recognition, Rethink Press and Jammy Digital. Small teams have infinite leverage in the times we are in and I'm proud to be working alongside you.

Thanks to you the reader for investing your time focus into this set of ideas.

ABOUT THE AUTHOR

Daniel Priestley is an entrepreneur, author, and keynote speaker who has spent more than two decades building and scaling businesses around the world. Starting his first company at the age of 21, Daniel went on to build, acquire and exit multiple ventures in software, publishing, agencies and business training.

He is the author of several bestselling books on business and entrepreneurship, including *Key Person of Influence*, *Oversubscribed*, *Entrepreneur Revolution* and *24 Assets*. His ideas have shaped the way thousands of entrepreneurs think about growing a businesses in the Digital Age.

As the co-founder of Dent Global, Daniel has worked with leaders and organizations across more than 50 industries, helping them to grow revenue, expand internationally and position themselves as market leaders. He has won several awards and been featured in Forbes and Entrepreneur.com.

Beyond entrepreneurship, Daniel is passionate about the education system and co-authored *How to Raise Entrepreneurial Kids*.

Daniel lives in London with his wife and three children.

INDEX

ALSO AVAILABLE BY
DANIEL PRIESTLEY

9780857089731

9780857088253

9781781331095

9781781332481

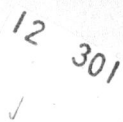